A GUIDE FOR SLEEP HEALTH AND SHIFTWORK

SLEEP4 PERFORMANCE

DR IAN C DUNICAN
DR TIM D SMITHIES

Published in Australia by Melius Consulting

M=LIUS
C O N S U L T I N G

First published in Australia 2024
This edition published by Melius Consulting 2024
Copyright © Ian Dunican and Tim D Smithies 2024

Cover design, typesetting: WorkingType (www.workingtype.com.au)

ISBN: 978-1-7636564-4-4

A catalogue record for this
book is available from the
National Library of Australia

Table of Contents

Figures

i. Author Biographies

Ian Charles Dunican
PhD, MBA, MMineEng, GCASSc, BA

1978–

Ian Dunican was born and raised in Ireland. Ian joined the Irish Army and was in an Infantry unit. After leaving the military, he spent two years working in the health and fitness industry and moved to Perth, Western Australia.

Ian worked in the mining industry for ten years in Australia and worldwide in health, safety, fatigue, human performance and business improvement. Whilst working full-time and travelling from Perth, he completed his undergraduate degree (Bachelor of Arts: Training and Development), Masters in Business, Masters in Mining Engineering and a Graduate degree in Adult Sleep Science. In 2014, Ian undertook his PhD at the University of Western Australia. He worked with the Australian Institute of Sport and the Western Force investigating Sleep and Performance in Elite Combat and Contact Athletes.

He is the Director and Chief Adviser of Melius Consulting, a scientific consultancy undertaking research, consulting, and education. Melius Consulting works across industrial businesses such as mining, oil and gas, rail, energy, media, emergency services, and aviation. They work with elite athletic organisations and athletes in Formula 1, Basketball, Combat Sports, Rugby, and Major League Baseball.

He is an Adjunct Senior Research Fellow at the University of Western Australia. In addition, he is involved in numerous research projects related to sport, shiftwork, nutrition, safety, death, and psychology and regularly publishes in academic journals. He hosts the Sleep4Performance Podcast and enjoys exploring philosophy, psychology, martial arts, culture, history, existential risk, and anything relevant to navigating a well-lived life.

Tim David Smithies
PhD, BSc (Hons)

1996–

Tim D Smithies is a scientific consultant at Melius Consulting. Tim's fascination with sleep started in his early teens, when he would get so nervous the night before his junior cricket matches that he would sometimes not sleep at all.

In 2014, Tim began his undergraduate degree at the University of Western Australia. He initially studied physiology and sports science; however, he ended up completing his degree in neuroscience & psychology. He then completed his Honours degree in 2017, working alongside the Western Force, exploring long-distance travel and its impact on sleep and performance. After spending the next 1.5 years living in Canada and the United Kingdom, Tim began his PhD at the Esports Science Research Lab at the University of Limerick (Ireland) on an industry-based project alongside Logitech. He completed this in 2023 and returned to Western Australia.

Tim is a Scientific Consultant at Melius Consulting, primarily involved in shift & roster design, sleep education and training, research & solutions, and data analysis/ visualisation. Additionally, Tim is an Adjunct Lecturer at the Appleton Institute, Central Queensland University. He is currently involved in research projects on shift & roster design, jet lag, sleep in sports, sleep and electronic devices, and sleep health. He is also the Project Manager of the Sleep Health Athletic Research Project (SHARP), a committee member of the Australian Sleep Association (ASA) Network of Early Career Sleep Researchers in Training (NEST), and the ASA Conference Committee. Tim has published and reviewed for many peer-review journals, written for scientific communication websites, and been a scientific communicator within national government-led health campaigns. He has also been a keynote speaker and a presenter at multiple international scientific conferences.

ii. Disclaimer

The information in this book on sleep health and shift workers' education is intended for general knowledge and educational purposes only. It is not a substitute for professional medical advice, diagnosis, or treatment. The content herein is based on research, expert opinion, and the author's experience; however, individual health conditions vary, and what may be beneficial for one person may not be suitable for another.

The contents of this book should not be used as a basis for any medical treatment. Always seek the advice of your physician or other qualified healthcare providers with any questions you may have regarding a medical condition, sleep disorder, or fatigue-related issue. Never disregard professional medical advice or delay in seeking it because of something you have read in this book.

The authors make no representations or warranties regarding the accuracy, applicability, or completeness of the information contained in this book. They expressly disclaim any responsibility for any adverse effects, outcomes, or consequences resulting from using or applying any information or recommendations provided herein.

iii. Endorsements and Foreword

Foreword

As a seasoned fatigue-management scientist and consultant, I have witnessed firsthand the challenges shift workers face in various fields, including those faced by shift workers in a variety of fields, including aviation, medicine, the military, mining, and others. Dr. Dunican's and Dr. Smithies' comprehensive exploration of sleep health within the vast shift-worker population represents a significant contribution to the field. Sleep Health for Shiftworkers is informative and empowering, offering practical strategies for individuals and organizations to improve sleep, manage sleep disorders, reduce fatigue, and enhance overall productivity, safety, and well-being.

Dr John Caldwell, PhD Experimental Psychologist, Fatigue Management Scientist and Consultant.

Endorsements

"Sleep is the foundation of our physical and mental well-being, yet many people suffer from sleep problems and disorders that can wreak havoc on their health. From insomnia and sleep apnea to restless leg syndrome and circadian rhythm disruptions, untreated sleep disorders can lead to fatigue, mood disturbances, impaired cognitive function, and increased risk of cardiovascular diseases. By understanding the causes and impacts of sleep problems and disorders and learning effective treatment strategies, you can reclaim your nights and restore balance to your life"

Dr David Cunnington, Sleep Physician and Scientist.

"Shiftworkers face unique challenges in maintaining their health and well-being. Sleep Health for Shiftworkers is a comprehensive guide designed specifically for those who work irregular hours, offering practical strategies to manage fatigue, improve sleep quality, and enhance overall physical and mental well-being. Drawing on the latest sleep science and chronobiology research, this book explores the physiological and psychological impacts of shift work, providing actionable tips for optimising rest in the most challenging schedules within the mining, oil and gas, emergency services or healthcare industries."

Dr Gemma Maisey. PhD Fatigue Risk Management and Scientist in the Mining Industry.

"As the General Manager of mining operations, sleep, shiftwork, and fatigue management are critical in a 24/7/365 operational environment. Our industry is demanding, and our operations' safety and efficiency heavily depend on every team member's well-being. Fatigue is one of the most significant risk factors in mining operations. It can lead to impaired judgment, slower reaction times, and a higher likelihood of accidents. Proper sleep and fatigue management are essential in reducing the risk of incidents that could endanger lives and disrupt operations. Education of employees on the importance of sleep health for shiftworkers is key to reducing risk and protecting people."

Josh Bennett, General Manager Operations and Mining Engineer.

Sleep Health for Shiftworkers is a groundbreaking resource that fills a critical gap in the available literature on the health and productivity of shift workers and, for that matter, anyone engaged in one of the thousands of occupations critical to the world's economy. In this text, Drs Dunican and Smithies have meticulously detailed clear, easy-to- read, and practical advice that will prove invaluable to workers and not only to workers themselves, but to those responsible for their employment and well-being. It is a must-read for anyone seeking to optimize sleep and performance in today's demanding 24/7 work environments.

Dr John Caldwell, PhD Experimental Psychologist, Fatigue Management Scientist and Consultant.

*"Sleeping is no mean art: for its sake
one must stay awake all day"*

Friedrich Nietzsche

Source: Friedrich Nietzsche by Edvard Munch
(Thielska Galleriet) – 1906 painting.

iv. Resources

Visit us at Sleep4Performance for more information. We have >130 podcast episodes, there are three seminars featuring more than 30 speakers, a variety of blogs and much more.

www.sleep4performance.com.au

Or, if you would like to know more about our consulting and educational services, go to www.meliusconsulting.com.au or email info@meliusconsulting.com.au

Melus Consulting is a scientific consultancy that specialises in

- Designing Fatigue Risk Management Systems

- Fitness for Work

- Education, Training and Health Promotion

- Shift and Roster Design

- Sleep Disorder Management Systems

- Applied Research and Industrial Studies

- Project and Change Management

- Health and Safety Technology Assessments and Deployment

Our clients include Rio Tinto, BHP, CBH Group, South32, Peabody Energy, Fugro, South Australia Power Networks, Shark Bay Salt, Woodside, Karara Mining, IGO, Refining NZ, Anglo Gold Ashanti Australia, Mineral Resources, Nine Entertainment, Fire Rescue Victoria, AusNet, Metro Trains Melbourne, Monash Health, Austin Health, CHC helicopters and many more.

v. Acronyms, Abbreviations and Definitions

i.i   Sleep, fatigue & circadian rhythms – general

AASM: The American Academy of Sleep Medicine.

"C" process: The circadian rhythm input within the two-process model.

Chronotype: Individual differences in time-of-day preferences for sleep/wake and other behaviours.

Circadian rhythm: A near 24 hr rhythm that is present in all humans and bears some influence on most (if not all) bodily processes.

Eating jet lag: Large variations in eating windows between days (i.e. between weekdays and weekends). Has been linked to weight gain.

ICSD: International Classification of Sleep Disorders.

Jet lag: Fatigue, sleep disturbances, and other symptoms associated with travel across three or more time zones. Caused by a mismatch between one's body clock and the light/dark cycle of the destination.

NREM: Non-rapid eye movement (sleep), stages of sleep not characterised by rapid eye movements.

Post-lunch dip: Sometimes called the "mid-afternoon dip". This is a period in the early afternoon (between 1 PM and 3 PM for most people), where alertness dips and sleepiness increases. This coincides with a siesta time within some cultures.

REM: Rapid eye movement (sleep), stage of sleep characterised by rapid eye movements.

"S" process: The sleep regulation or sleep pressure input within the two-process model. Increases while awake and decreases while asleep.

Social jet lag: Large sleep and wake timing variations due to social factors (e.g., between weekdays and weekends) leading to fatigue and other symptoms.

Travel fatigue: Fatigue, sleep disturbances, and other symptoms associated with travel, however *not* due to travel across time zones.

WMZ: Wake maintenance zone (also sometimes called the forbidden zone). Usually 2-3 hrs before habitual bedtime. The time in which circadian alertness is at its peak and right before melatonin secretion begins. Alertness, reaction time and physical performance are normally high, and the ability to nap or sleep is normally low.

WOCL: Window of circadian low, The time of day in which circadian alertness is at its lowest and circadian drive to sleep is at its highest. Usually around 03:00 to 06:00 for most people.

i.ii   Sleep measurements

Actigraphy: Wearable sleep measurement device. Usually worn on the wrist.

EEG: Electroencephalography, A device used to measure the brain's electrical activity.

EMG: Electromyography, A device used to measure the electrical activity of muscles.

EOG: Electrooculography, A device used to measure the electrical activity of the eyes.

PSG: Polysomnography is the current "gold standard" of sleep measurement and is used to diagnose many sleep disorders. It includes EEG, EOG, EMG, breathing measurements, oxygen levels, snoring, and body position measures. Normally completed in a hospital or sleep laboratory, however, at-home versions are becoming increasingly available.

SE: Sleep efficiency, the total sleep time divided by time in bed, multiplied by 100.

SOL: Sleep onset latency, the number of minutes from time at lights out to the time of sleep onset.

TASO: Time at Sleep Onset, the time of day at which a person falls asleep.

TAW: Time at Wake, the time a person wakes with no further sleep.

TIB: Time in bed, the total time spent in bed, from lights out until time at wake).

TST: Total sleep time, the number of minutes from the time of sleep onset to the last awakening, minus the number of minutes awake during this period.

WASO: Time awake after sleep onset, number of minutes awake, between the time of sleep onset and last awakening.

i.iii   Sleep disorders

Bruxism: Disorder involving the clenching of teeth, often during sleep.

CBT-I: Cognitive Behavioural Therapy for Insomnia, a psychology-based treatment for insomnia.

CPAP: Continuous positive airway pressure. A device that acts as a pneumatic splint, helping to keep the airway open during sleep.

Insomnia: A sleep disorder characterised by an inability to fall asleep or remain asleep for an adequate length of time.

MAS: Mandibular advancement splint, a device worn in the mouth which acts as a mechanical splint, keeping the airway open.

Narcolepsy: A sleep disorder characterised by extreme daytime tiredness and often involuntary sleep.

OSA: Obstructive sleep apnea (or apnoea), A sleep disorder characterised by partial or complete airway collapses or obstructions, leading to awakenings or reduction in oxygen saturation levels (or both).

PLM: Periodic limb movement disorders, unusual leg movements that affect sleep by causing disruptions and lowering sleep duration and quality.

RBD: REM behaviour disorder, a sleep disorder in which muscle atonia (or paralysis) normally experienced in REM sleep ceases to occur.

RLS: Restless leg syndrome, uncontrollable urge to move legs while sitting or lying down.

SWD: Shift work disorder, insomnia symptoms and excessive sleepiness occurring in response to abnormal work hours.

i.iv   Other

ADHD: Attention-deficit/hyperactivity disorder.

ASD: Autism spectrum disorder.

BAC: Blood Alcohol Concentrate.

BMI: Body Mass Index.

CBD: Cannabidiol, a cannabinoid present in cannabis. It does not produce psychoactive effects.

CVD: Cardiovascular disease.

GP: General Practitioner.

Hr: Hour.

Kg: Kilogram.

Meta-analysis: a statistical examination of data on a particular topic, which has been collected from multiple studies.

Min: Minute.

Pharmacokinetics: What the body does to a drug. As opposed to pharmacodynamics, which is what a drug does to the body.

PTSD: Post-traumatic stress disorder.

THC: Δ9-tetrahydrocannabinol, a cannabinoid present in cannabis. It is responsible for the psychoactive effect of cannabis.

WHO: World Health Organisation.

VO$_2$ max: maximal oxygen consumption, a measure of cardiovascular fitness.

°C: Degrees Celcius (temperature).

<: Less than.

>: Greater than

~: Approximate

vi. Acknowledgements

Before we delve into the topic of sleep, I would like to thank, as always, my wife, who supports me in my vast array of interests and distractions. Dr Tim D Smithies who has earned a co-author spot on this book due to his contributions in generating the content, checking for corrections and identifying ways to promote our content.

Dr John Caldwell for his friendship, scientific support and contributions to this text via the development of blogs and other scientific writings. To Mr Phil Beranek, who contributed to the section on managing sleep in relation to sleep environment.

We extend our thanks to the team members at Melius Consulting. Their dedication and commitment to providing education excellence and consulting to a wide variety of projects and customers is truly commendable.

We appreciate the contributions and support of Dr Clare Ladyman, Holly Fraser, Dr Mitchell Turner, Dr Travis Cruickshank, Martha Cavanagh, Sarah Mutch, Neill Maderia, Dr Cele Richardson, and Nicola Ward for business support, and Rachel Huber for media and website expertise.

Finally, to all my scientific collaborators and students who have enriched my continuing development as a scientist, to all the guests on the podcasts who have provided invaluable one-on-one educational sessions for me, and to all the students who have taken our courses and have provided valuable feedback.

Dr Ian Dunican *PhD, MBA, MMineEng, GCASSc, BA.*

Director and Chief Adviser, Melius Consulting and Sleep4Performance

1. Introduction

Welcome to *A guide for sleep health and shiftwork,* a concise guide born from years of expertise and passion. We have finally brought this long-planned book project to life. Whether you are part of our online or face-to-face education training programs, or simply exploring sleep health, this book offers invaluable insights into the intricacies of sleep science, chronobiology, sleep disorders, shift work, jet lag, and more.

This book is an extension of our *Sleep Health and Fatigue Management* courses, yet it is a comprehensive resource. While there's overlap, not every topic in this book is covered in the course and vice versa. Together, they form a holistic learning experience. However, reading this book alone will enrich your understanding of sleep health.

The field of sleep science is ever evolving, with research spanning diverse areas like sleep in athletes, shift workers, education, healthcare, mining, oil and gas, dreams, nightmares, anxiety, emergency services, and more. This book is not an exhaustive guide but a stepping stone towards better sleep and well-being. For further information and resources, visit our website, Sleep4Performance.com.au, where you can access over 100 podcasts, years of seminars, blogs, and videos.

Writing this book presented unique challenges in trying to balance the input of academic and consulting knowledge. Our goal was to take scientific knowledge, often confined to academic circles, and make it accessible to everyone—especially those with demanding jobs, irregular schedules, or a keen interest in improving their sleep health.

With over 200 scientific references, this book is grounded in the latest research and our professional experience across many industries. It is evidence-based on research and practical application. I hope you find it informative, thought-provoking, and, ultimately, beneficial to your sleep and overall health. As the science progresses, so will future editions of this book. Start with section one to build a solid foundation and enjoy your journey into the fascinating world of sleep health.

Sleep Science and Circadian Rhythms

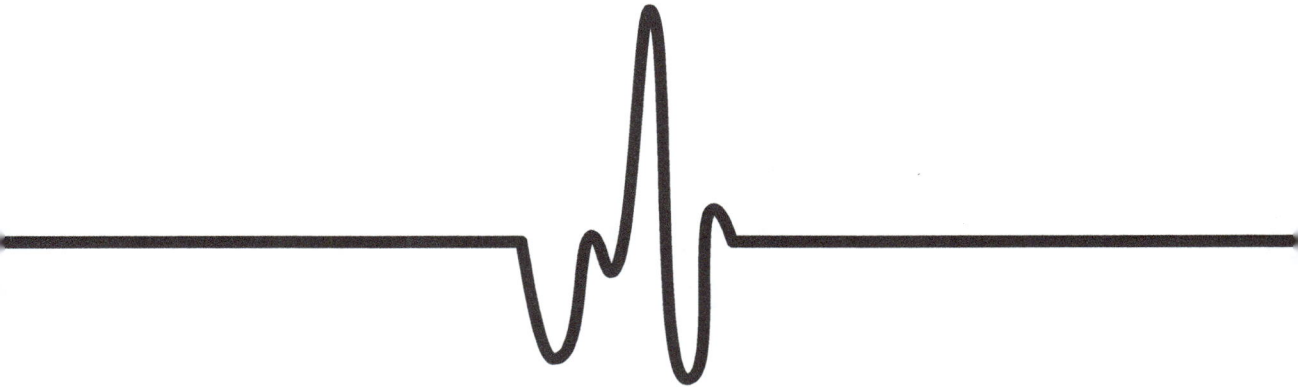

2. Sleep Science and Circadian Rhythms

2.1 Why do we sleep?

In truth, we still do not know the one reason why we sleep. Many research studies have shown that bad outcomes occur when we restrict, deprive, or force humans to lose sleep. Sleep is critical for human survival and human body functioning, including body temperature regulation,[1, 2] and immune function[3]. We do know that sleep is a process that supports the recovery of both body and brain to enable next-day physical[4] and cognitive performance[5].

Loss of sleep (less than 7 hrs per night) can lead to loss of attention[6, 7], poor reaction time[8], and overall reduction in cognitive performance, including executive functioning or your ability to think[6,8]. This means that you are likely to make poorer decisions and make them more slowly when you have lost sleep.

Every year, more and more researchers join the world of sleep research from a wide variety of disciplines, so our knowledge in this area continues to grow. These researchers go on to specialise in different aspects of sleep research, such as:

- Sleep disorder research

- Laboratory-based sleep research

- Applied sleep and chronobiology research with applications for shiftworkers or elite athletes

- Mathematicians and statisticians modelling the relationship between sleep and performance

- Circadian rhythms, human functioning and performance

- Economists quantifying the impact of poor sleep

Every day, our knowledge of human sleep and, thus, our ability to overcome sleep-related issues improves, and by reading this, you are supporting this process. But to truly understand where we are going in the sleep science field, we must go back and explore where it all started. Let us look at the history of sleep in humans.

2.2   Brief history of sleep science in humans

The precise function of sleep has puzzled the scientific and philosophical community for over 2,000 years. In early Greek philosophy, we see mention of sleep made by several prominent Philosophers.

Heraclitus (535–475 BCE) said,

"For those awake, there is a common universe, whereas in sleep, each person turns away into his private universe".

This is true, as we have unique dreams that no one can observe when we sleep.

HERACLITVS.

Figure 1. Heraclitus, ancient Greek Philosopher from Thomas Stanley 1655

Empedocles (490-430 BCE) hypothesised that sleep occurred due to the blood's partial or *"proportionate"* cooling and that if your blood completely cooled off, you would die.

Plato (427-347 BCE) believed that we can see because we can emit a non-burning, light-giving, *"pure fire"* from our eyes and strike external objects. However, at night time, this *"pure fire"* departs, both ceasing our ability to see and driving us towards sleep.

In 350 BCE, **Aristotle** developed the first scientific theory of sleep. He hypothesised that we become sleepy or fall asleep due to *"vapours from the food we consumed"* [9], and that sleep functions to help us digest food. He further hypothesised that we wake up from sleep when digestion is complete [9]. Such food-related hypotheses continued for over 1,500 years through to the Middle Ages.

In 1729, the first recorded observations of biological rhythms came from a French scientist **Jean Jacques tortuous de Marian,** who was intrigued by the mimosa plant's daily opening and closing pattern. De Marian placed the plant in a constantly dark room for several days. He observed that the plants continued to open and close according to a 24 hr pattern (or a diurnal pattern), even without sunlight[10]. This observation would pave the way for the discovery of circadian rhythms in humans[10,11].

Much of our modern understanding of how sleep affects our physiology can be attributed to the electroencephalogram (EEG) invention in the 1930s. Before this, the belief and scientific knowledge of sleep was that it was a passive or a *"quiet"* state, which is inevitable following the amount of information received throughout the day and the resulting depletion of brain activity[12].

In 1937, **Alfred Lee Loomis**[13] discovered that during sleep, electrical waves generated by the brain slowed and became larger in amplitude compared to when awake. Further understanding of sleep physiology came in 1952 when Eugene Aserinsky placed EEG electrodes near the eyes of a sleeping child and observed regular bursts of electrical activity[14].

This led **Eugene Aserinsky and Nathaniel Kleitman** to coin the phrase Rapid Eye Movement (REM), considered the *"time for dreaming",* with REM periods occurring on average every 90 mins. It was further shown that during REM sleep, brain activity increases to a level that is similar to that during wake[13, 15]. This discovery led to the development of sleep stages by **Allan Rechtschaffen and Anthony Kales**, who categorised sleep into distinct REM and non-REM (NREM) sleep stages.

These significant milestones, alongside countless other discoveries, have led to continual growth in human sleep knowledge. Unfortunately, while our understanding of sleep improves, new challenges for improving or optimising human sleep continue to surface in parallel. A significant cause of these challenges has been the discovery of electricity, the invention of artificial light, and its inescapable presence in modern society. Whilst it has supported industrialisation, economic development, and growth, how does it impact our sleep?

2.3   Electricity and shiftwork

Electricity has allowed us to light up the night and keep working. This significant technological change has enabled shiftwork and working at odd hours at the scale that it exists today. Establishing when shiftwork begins can be difficult; however, it precedes artificial light. Nomadic people may have needed to stay awake and alert during some hours of the night to tend to animals or to defend themselves from

Figure 2. Lighting of a gas lamp

Figure note: Gas lighting. (2024, July 15). In *Wikipedia*. https://en.wikipedia.org/wiki/Gas_lighting

Want to know more about the history of sleep?   ?

Season 3, Episode 2: The History of Sleep with Prof Roger Ekirch. In this episode, Ian had the privilege of talking with the great Professor Roger Ekirch. Roger Ekirch is an award-winning author and University Distinguished Professor in the Department of History at Virginia Tech. His work is related to the history of "segmented sleep" before the twentieth century. It has changed how we think about sleep. A member of the editorial board of Sleep Health: The Journal of the National Sleep Foundation, he has given keynote addresses to medical gatherings in Kyoto, Cambridge (United Kingdom), Göttingen, Washington, D.C., Richmond, Denver, and in London at the Royal Society of Medicine, as well as grand rounds talks to medical staff at Roanoke Memorial Hospital and the Virginia Hospital Center in Arlington. Roger was a great guest on the podcast, and it was a joy to talk to Roger about the history of sleep. We discussed the change in how we sleep since the Industrial Revolution and how we may not sleep so well since the invention of electricity.

LISTEN HERE:

https://sleep4performance.com/podcast/s4p-radio-season-3-episode-2-the-history-of-sleep/

OR SCAN QR CODE

predators. In the Roman army, soldiers used torches to light up the area around a barracks or fort to stand guard at night, and sailors and explorers conducted watch periods. It is thought that during the Renaissance in Europe (circa 1490-1520s), construction took place on a 24/7 basis.

During the Industrial Revolution in Britain (1760-1840), gas lamps were used in homes, streets and workplaces to allow for work throughout the evening and night. As human use of electricity became more widespread, more industries began to use shiftwork to maximise operating time and increase return on investment. With the widespread use of electricity and the internet, shiftwork and irregular work has become somewhat normalised today. Workers are continuously connected to their workplace.

Sleep and how much sleep do we need?

On average, humans will spend approximately one-third of their lives asleep. The life expectancy in Australia is 83; the United States (US) is 77; and the United Kingdom (UK) is 81. Therefore, the average

- Australians will spend 27.6 years asleep

- Americans will spend 25.6 years asleep

- The British will spend 27 years asleep

Scientific insight: world record attempt for staying awake 👁

From December to January of 1963-64, a seventeen-year-old school kid called Randy Gardner went without sleep for 11 days or 264 hrs. Observed by the late esteemed scientist Dr William Dement, Randy did not consume any stimulants or take any medications to reduce his sleepiness during the experiment. This became a world record. However, the Guinness World Records no longer endorses, sanctions, or recognises new attempts for fear of ill effects. On completion, Randy slept for almost 15 hrs, with a further 10.5 hrs of sleep the following night, and very quickly recovered any lost capacity due to the sleep loss. It must be noted that Randy was 17 years old, had no commitments, was not working and did not have children or a mortgage.

As stated earlier, we sleep for many reasons, and it is extremely important for our health and longevity. Not achieving enough sleep can have short and long-term adverse effects, some of which we will discuss later.

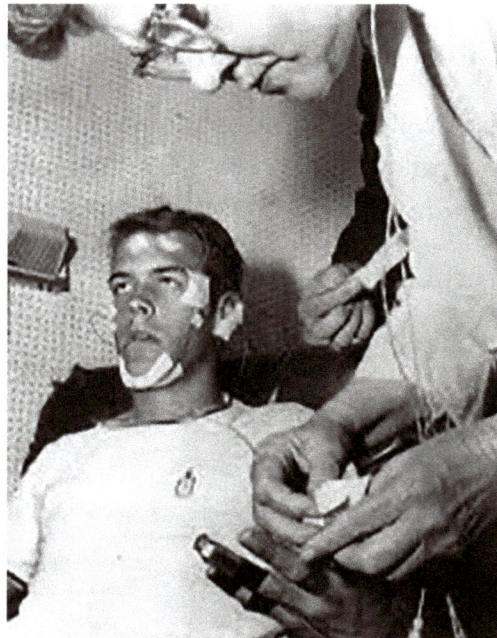

Figure 3. Randy Gardner
Guinness World Record Attempt

2.4   Sleep loss in today's world

The way we live has changed with the increase of modern technologies, high-speed travel, and the internet being available at our fingertips 24 hrs a day. However, unfortunately, it is quite clear that our sleep has not adapted to the demands of the modern world, and we have not evolved to cope with such changes. We are worse at achieving sleep than we were in the 1970s. According to Deloitte Access Economics and the Sleep Health Foundation[16] in Australia, which has produced a series of reports since 2010, approximately 4 in 10 Australians continuously report insufficient sleep throughout the week.

Figure 4. Sleep Problems in Australia

Sleep loss is when we do not achieve 7-9 hrs of recommended sleep per night. This may occur for several reasons, including a lousy night's sleep, which is not unusual and can happen on several nights a month. These poor nights of sleep can be due to many factors, such as:

- Stress

- Increases in physical activity

- Suboptimal sleep habits and behaviours

- Presence of a sleep disorder

- Health conditions

- Alcohol or caffeine

- Medications

Many people who commonly experience sleep loss aim to catch up on lost sleep the following night or on the weekend. However, this is not always possible, especially as increasing sleep duration can be difficult on the weekends usually as people go to bed later and do not extend their time in bed enough to catch up on lost sleep throughout the week.

2.5   Reflection on sleep duration each night

You can estimate your sleep by keeping a sleep diary for the next seven nights or using a wearable device that measures sleep. Total the number of hours less than 7 hrs per night to calculate your sleep loss for the seven nights. The example here shows the sleep duration achieved each night for 7 nights (Monday to Sunday):

Monday night	7 hrs	
Tuesday night	8 hrs	
Wednesday	5 hrs	(-2 hrs)
Thursday	6 hrs	(-1 hr)
Friday	7 hrs	
Saturday	8 hrs	
Sunday	6 hrs	(-1 hr)

Total sleep loss = 4 hrs over 7 days

Average sleep duration across the week (7 nights) is 6 hrs 43 mins

Sleep deprivation is not sleeping (or staying awake) for 24 hrs or longer. Typically, this happens in laboratory-based studies but has real-world applications. In specific jobs such as firefighting or emergency response, medical/surgical roles, utilities, and military, it is not uncommon to be awake for longer than 24 consecutive hrs and up to 96 hrs for operational reasons such as emergency services. Throughout this book, we will discuss the impact of sleep deprivation (also sometimes called extended wakefulness) on health, safety, cognitive and physical performance.

In response to sleep deprivation experienced within an occupational setting, some may say,

"Just don't work those hours" or *"Just say no to your boss"*

We have heard this at scientific conferences from medical practitioners or academics. While these responses may seem sensible according to *"scientific best practice"*, they lack reality. Suppose an operational military platoon is in a combat environment. They cannot simply raise a flag and say to their adversary,

"Stop, we have reached the working hours limit."

Or perhaps, think about firefighters fighting a building blaze during an emergency or extracting a casualty from a car wreckage. They will not stop the job and say they can't work because they have been awake for too long. You may be thinking of multiple incidents where this has occurred, and sometimes, we must battle through and contend with these unfortunate circumstances.

Sleep restriction is when we are not provided with a sleep opportunity conducive to our 7-9 hrs of sleep per night. Suppose you only have 7 hrs between two work shifts. How are you expected to get 8 hrs of sleep, eat, exercise, attend to personal hygiene, and spend time with family and friends? It is not possible. This is often described as a simple mathematical issue. You may also impose sleep restrictions on yourself by not allowing enough *"time in bed"*. This may be from staying up late each night or exercising exceptionally early. This may be impacted by your chronotype, which we will discuss later.

2.6 Reflection on your sleep loss

You can estimate your levels of sleep restriction by analysing your work pattern. Have a look at the total hours for rest and recovery between shifts. Generally, this should be at least 10 hrs to allow for commuting to and from work, time for sleep, time to eat, exercise, attending to personal hygiene, and spending time with family and friends. If not, your work hour design/ shift and roster system may need attention.

Want to know more about sleep in the military? ?

Season 2, Episode 2: Sleep is a Weapon with special guest: Bram Connolly, CEO of Hindsight Crisis Management & Founder & President of Warrior U. Bram spent 20 years in the Australian Defence Force, 15 years of which were spent in the Australian Special Forces and was awarded the Distinguished Service Medal for leadership in combat in 2012. Bram is the CEO of Hindsight Crisis Management and the founder and president of Warrior U (Pty Ltd), an enterprise that seeks to mobilise and motivate the next generation as well as an accomplished public speaker, tackling such topics as PTSD, Veteran victimisation and the changing face of terrorism. His position on these topics is underpinned by a Bachelor of International Studies at the University of New England (UNE), majoring in societies and peace studies. Bram is the author of *"The Fighting Season" and "Off-Reservation",* both published by Allen and Unwin in 2016 and 2017, respectively.

LISTEN HERE:

https://sleep4performance.com/podcast/major-bram-connolly-dsm-australian-commandos/

OR SCAN QR CODE

Example: A nurse who works an evening shift from 16:00 (4 pm) to 00:00 (midnight) and then returns for a morning shift at 08:00. When we factor in commute to and from work, time to eat, time to shower and time to wind down, this may only leave <6 hrs of time for sleep (if they're lucky).

Myths about sleep training: You cannot train yourself to get by on less sleep. Some people say that in the military, this is what they do; no, it isn't. The sleep loss, deprivation or restriction in the military is to mimic real combat events and to practice and apply systems under this duress. The main purpose here is to familiarise the operative with the stress of the condition.

2.7   But how much sleep do we need?

You may have heard that a human needs between 7-9 hrs sleep per night to function during the day (mainly because we also wrote this earlier!). You may also have heard that we need less sleep as we age. But are these statements factual, or is there more to it? The National Sleep Foundation[17] in the United States recommends that adults between the ages of 18-64 obtain 7-9 hrs of sleep per night, and that those 65 or over should obtain 7-8 hrs of sleep per night. It is estimated that less than 1% of people are biologically programmed to only need <5 hrs of sleep even though many people may think they only need this amount.

The challenge with these recommendations is that humans are not like machines, and we do not always get enough sleep due to biological, behavioural, or environmental reasons. Furthermore, even within these age brackets, there is large individual variability, meaning you may need more (or less) sleep than your peers. Therefore, these recommendations should serve as a general guide. It may be best to reflect on sleep duration over a 7 or 21 day period, as night-to-night variation can occur.

Scientific insight: the importance of regular sleep patterns

In a large-scale study led by Lachlan Cribb and friends investigating sleep regularity and mortality using the UK biobank data with >88,000 people, researchers examined the relationship between sleep regularity (consistency of sleep and wake timing), risk of all-cause, cardiovascular disease (CVD), and cancer mortality. They found that mortality rates were highest in persons with the most irregular sleep and decreased as sleep regularity improved. The data indicated a relationship between sleep regularity and longevity in a large community-based cohort. In this analysis, the relationship between sleep regularity and longevity was even greater than the relationship between sleep duration and longevity! Therefore, a consistent sleep routine is essential for your overall health [18].

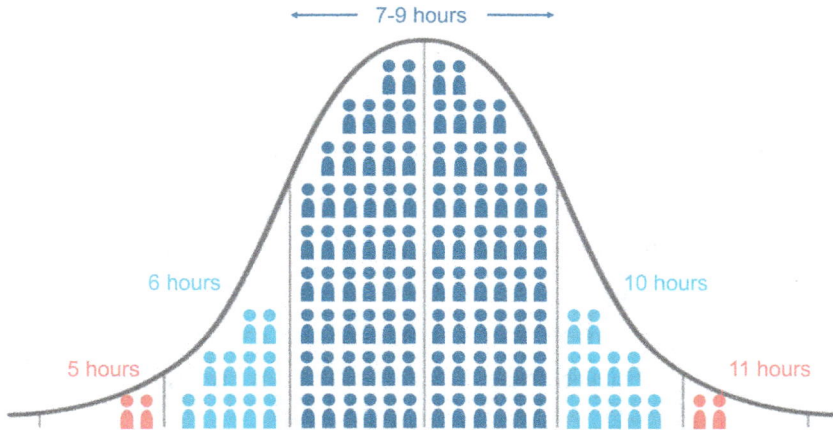

Figure 5. Sleep Duration Needs

2.8   What are sleep stages?

Sleep is classified into two distinct types: Rapid Eye Movement (REM) and Non-Rapid Eye Movement (NREM). These classifications include specific stages of sleep that have been categorised according to the American Academy of Sleep Medicine (AASM) criteria. In this system,

- **NREM** sleep consists of two light stages of sleep (N1 and N2) and a deeper stage of sleep, slow wave sleep (N3).

- **REM** is just one stage. This is where most (~80%) of our dreaming occurs.

Specific changes in brain activity, breathing rate, and movement of the eyes and body characterise each stage. During a typical 8 hr sleep period, an individual will spend 5% in N1, 50% in N2, 20% in N3, and 25% in REM. Humans cycle through the lighter stages of sleep (N1) to the deeper stages (N3), and then back to the lighter stages (N1, REM, and sometimes wake!) in a predictable manner; these are called sleep cycles. The first sleep cycle lasts between 70 and 100 mins, with subsequent sleep cycles lasting 90-120 mins in adults (sleep cycles are shorter in babies and children). NREM sleep is prioritised early in the sleep period, while REM sleep tends to occur later in the sleep period. These sleep cycles can change each night. Your body is not a machine whereby it jumps to a different stage on a time cue, nor can you influence the amount of time you spend in each stage. The main ways to impact these are to spend more time in bed, reduce or eliminate drugs and alcohol, exercise, eliminate caffeine after 2 pm, and get light exposure during the day, all of which we will talk about throughout this book. You cannot implement one single countermeasure to increase a specific stage; it will be a holistic approach.

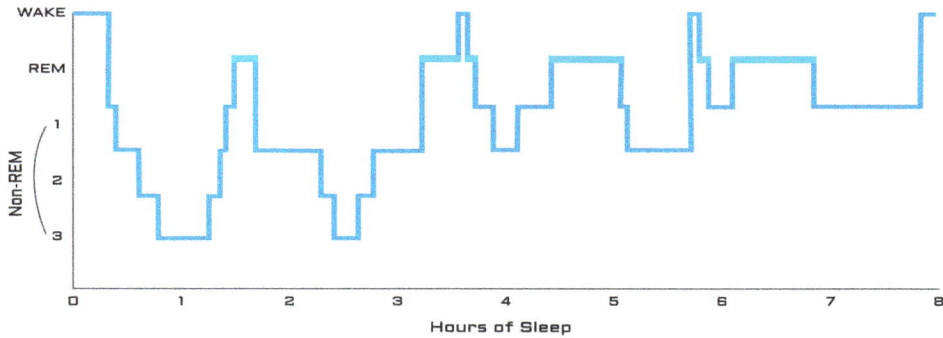

Figure 6. Example of Stages of Sleep

2.9   How is sleep regulated?

Sleep pressure: Sleep is regulated or controlled by two mechanisms known as the "S" process and the *"C"* process. The *"S process"* is sometimes called sleep regulation or sleep pressure. This drive for sleep increases with time awake. In conjunction with this, adenosine (a neurotransmitter or chemical within the brain) builds up, rising throughout the day or the longer we are awake. If a person does not achieve the optimal amount of sleep, then a sleep debt is carried forward, and the pressure builds upon this. Sleep pressure may increase due to sickness or engaging in cognitive or physically demanding tasks. Sleep pressure increases the more time is spent awake and decreases the more time is spent asleep. It is as simple as that. The cure for tiredness due to sustained hours of wakefulness is ...yes, you guessed correctly, SLEEP.

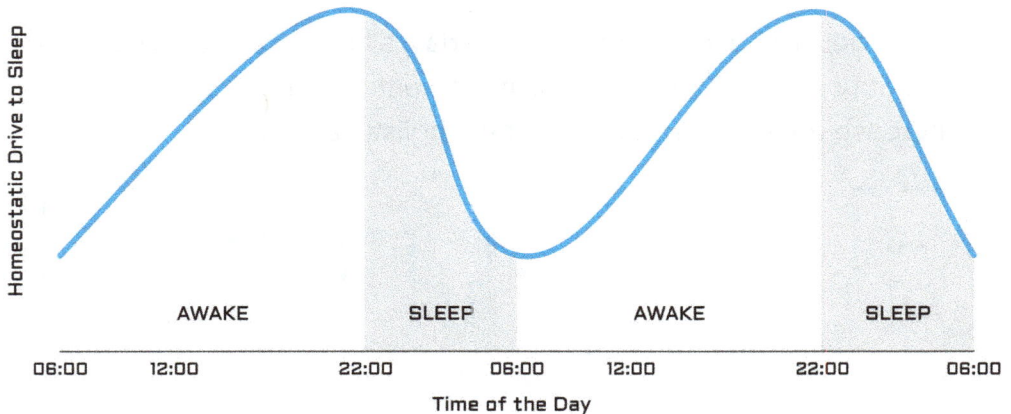

Figure 7. Sleep Pressure

Circadian rhythms: The *"C"* process is the circadian process. This is a biological rhythm that occurs over 24 hrs. The rhythmic pattern that pertains to sleep is a circadian rhythm. The word *"Circadian"* comes from the Latin words *"Circa"*, meaning *"about"*, and *"Dia"*, meaning *"a day"*, and describes our internal biological rhythms, which oscillate on a nearly 24 hr cycle[19]. Circadian rhythms are also present in animals and plants.

The human circadian rhythm is ultimately governed by the suprachiasmatic nuclei (SCN), a small part of the hypothalamus in the brain[20]. The SCN is often called the body's master clock, as it synchronises or coordinates many bodily processes, including

- Cardiovascular function

- Digestive functioning

- Respiratory processes

- Morning cortisol secretions

- Temperature[21]

- Metabolic changes[22]

Human circadian rhythms can be influenced by external inputs from the environment known as zeitgebers (i.e., time givers), such as mealtimes, social cues, and working time. Natural light (received through the eyes) is the greatest naturally occurring circadian zeitgeber, and receiving this light helps align the SCN or master clock to the Earth's solar day[23]. However, artificial light can also influence the human circadian rhythm.

Circadian rhythms govern our sleep-wake cycle. Within 24 hrs, the circadian system will typically promote wakefulness for 16 hrs, followed by the promotion of sleep for 8 hrs. The sleep-wake rhythm is also associated with rhythmic fluctuations in sleep-related hormones, whereby, upon waking, morning cortisol increases, and melatonin decreases[24, 25].

We experience the most significant dip in our circadian rhythm between 03:00-06:00 in the morning, often called the *"Window of Circadian Low"*, with low body temperature and difficulty staying alert when awake or working. In the afternoon (between 13:00-15:00 for most people), we experience a *"post-lunch dip"*. During this period, it can be challenging to maintain cognitive vigilance, and sleepiness tends to increase. In some cultures, such as Greek and Spanish, this is when many people have a siesta or short afternoon sleep period.

In the evening, approximately 2-3 hrs before bedtime, it is known as the *"forbidden zone"* or the Wake Maintenance Zone (WMZ)[26]. The WMZ is the most challenging time to sleep in a 24 hr period[27]. During the WMZ, cardiovascular efficiency and muscular strength tend to be at their peak. Later in the evening, progressing into the night, cortisol levels decline, and melatonin is produced from the pineal gland. In conjunction with increased sleep pressure, these processes result in the perfect storm for the onset of sleep.

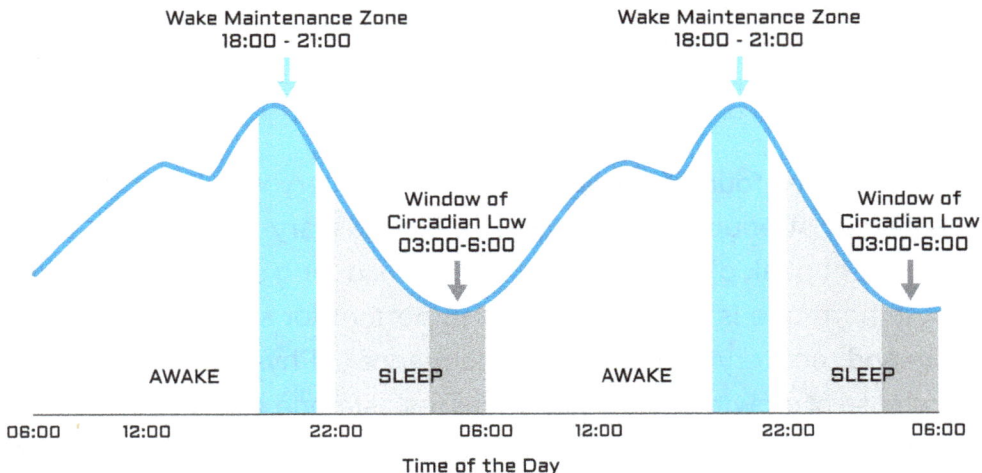

Figure 8. Window of Circadian Low and Wake Maintenance Zone

2.10 How does sleep impact my cognitive and physical performance?

In general, human cognitive performance or brain functioning is negatively affected by sleep loss. This is at least partly due to sustained hours of wakefulness. For example, suppose you are awake for 17 hrs. In that case, you will have the same reaction time as someone who is intoxicated to a level of 0.05% Blood Alcohol Concentrate (BAC)[28]. This is the legal limit in many countries.

Sleep restriction can also result in significant increases in reaction time and reduced cognitive performance, depending on the specific dose of sleep an individual has had. Studies have shown that having only a 4 hr or 6hr sleep opportunity per day, across many consecutive days, can result in negative impacts to reaction time that are comparable to what is experienced when you don't sleep at all for 1-2 days[6]. Additionally, the greater the sleep loss or the more days sleep loss is experienced on, the larger the negative impact.

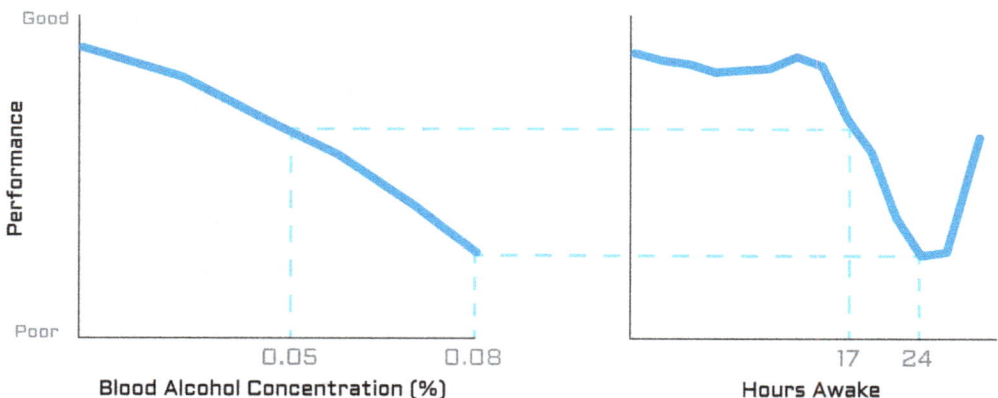

Figure 9. Sleep Loss and Performance Relation to Alcohol

Sleep has been found to support physical recovery in humans following exercise or strenuous work[29] and is a necessary process to enable subsequent peak physical performance. It is during stage N3 sleep that growth hormone is released. This is important for supporting physical repair and recovery for next-day performance[30]. Physical repair requires the release of growth hormones, such as testosterone, a crucial component for skeletal muscle and physical health and well-being in humans[31]. Sleep disruption leading to sleep loss will negatively affect the regulation of these growth hormones and other hormones, leading to poorer metabolic and endocrine functioning, including decreased glucose tolerance, insulin sensitivity, and increased evening cortisol[32]. In conjunction with growth hormone, appetite regulation is controlled by hormones such as leptin and ghrelin, which have been linked to the timing and duration of sleep[32].

2.11 What is a chronotype?

Chronotype is a term used to define a type of sleep/wake behaviour. It is not related to the amount of sleep you need, nor is your chronotype indicative if you are a short (<7 hrs), regular (7-9 hrs) or long sleeper (>9 hrs).

Chrono means *"time",* and type refers to one of the three types: morning (owl), intermediate and evening (lark). As the names suggest,

- Owls tend to go to bed late and get up late

- Intermediates tend to go to bed and wake up neither late nor early. They also tend to be able to change their sleep-wake behaviours relatively quickly, depending on social and environmental factors

- Larks tend to go to bed early and get up early

While people may be forced into an earlier routine (more suitable for a lark) due to their shiftwork or working regime, they may be more of an owl. That same person, however, is much more likely to better cope with night shifts than a lark. If you are intermediate, you can most likely adjust between different shiftwork regimes without many issues. If you are a lark, you may have to make considerable changes to work night shifts.

Chronotypes change and evolve over one's life. For example, when we are young children, we tend to be more of a lark chronotype, getting up early and going to bed early. Between the ages of 15-25, we change to an owl, often struggling to sleep until late at night and wanting to wake up later.

Once we become older adults (>65 years old), we tend more towards a lark chronotype. Hormonal and behavioural changes, such as getting up earlier, may affect this.

Scientific insight: chronotype distribution

In a 12-year study examining over 50,000 people, researchers found that 25% of people were larks, 25% were owls, and 50% were intermediate. The variability of chronotype also decreases with age; generally, after 40 years of age, we start to see more lark-type sleep behaviour [33].

2.12 How do I know my chronotype?

| Morning Lark | Intermediate Dove | Night Owl |
| Early to bed, early to rise | Flexible with bedtimes/waketimes | Late to bed, late to rise |

Figure 10. Chronotypes

There are several ways to assess a person's chronotype, including collecting sleep and wake behaviour over time (generally at least 7 nights) or using validated questionnaires such as the Munich Chronotype Questionnaire or the Horne-Ostberg's Morningness-Eveningness Score [34]. However, a more quick and straightforward way is to ask yourself the following question.

Reflection: What would be your ideal wake-up time if you didn't have to wake up for work and were on holiday with no alarm clock? Your choice may be indicative of your chronotype

	Definite evening	Moderate evening	Intermediate	Moderate morning	Definite morning
Wake up Time	10:00–11:30 am	08:30–10:00am	06:30–08:30am	05:00–06:30am	04:00–05:00am

2.13 How do I change between lark and owl?

Many people ask,

> *"How can I change between lark and owl, with many popular social media posts informing us of the potential benefits of being a morning person or a lark?"*

Firstly, becoming a morning person (lark) is not necessarily better for your sleep, recovery, health, and performance. If you are more of an owl, fighting against your biological clock may harm your performance. Despite what famous figures on YouTube or Podcasts say, you must optimise your routines to best suit yourself. Many of these individuals make valid points about discipline, planning, exercising, getting sunlight, and having a routine, all of which are vital regardless of whether you're a lark or an owl.

You may be a shift worker reading this and thinking,

> *"Is it possible to change lark to owl continuously for my rotating shift type?"*

In other words, can I switch to more of a lark for four day shifts and then to an owl for four night shifts? The answer, unfortunately, is no. Such rapid changes to one's sleep wake behaviours are impossible in applied real-life settings and certainly not for rotating shiftworkers. Humans tend to function at their best when they are on a consistent schedule, which aligns with their chronotype, perhaps with slight variations or changes from season to season.

Before you try to change from lark to an owl or vice versa, ask yourself,

> *"Do I need to change my sleep wake behaviours, or do I need to change my schedule?"*.

Chronotypes are largely biologically determined, so it can be challenging for many people to change their chronotype and then just as tricky to maintain a chronotype that does not match up with the person's biological drivers. Because of this difficulty, it is worthwhile asking yourself these questions before attempting a considerable change of routine.

- Do you need to change your sleep and wake pattern in the first place?

- Instead, can you alter your work hours to start and finish times?

- Can you instead move to a permanent shift type that may suit you?

- Can you move around your exercise and mealtimes instead of your bed/wake times?

Some minor changes may allow you to accomplish what you need to do without a change in chronotype.

Scientific insight: social jet lag and poor health

A study was conducted investigating social jet lag and depressive symptoms of 1,404 adults (18-78 years old) over four years. The research team collected self-reported information on sleep habits to determine the midpoint of sleep for weekdays and weekends or days off, and depression was measured using a validated scale. In addition, their dietary habits were assessed using a validated self-administered questionnaire. Based on the data, participants were assigned to a social jet lag category, ranging from least (≤1 hr) and middle (1-2 hr) to highest (≥2 hr) amount of social jet lag. The participants in the ≥ 2 hr category (high social jet lag) were more likely to be younger, female, blue-collar workers with a lower average income, who smoked and were more likely to be an owl chronotype. The team found a relationship linking social jetlag to an increased likelihood of having depressive symptoms. They also consumed lower amounts of vitamin C, calcium, magnesium, iron, and folate [35].

Want to know more about chronotypes?

?

Season 7 Episode 8: Sleep Quality, Phenotypes, Chronotypes and Diurnal Preferences with Dr Nicola Barclay. Nicola Barclay, PhD, is a Sleep Scientist and Psychologist with extensive experience in sleep research, research design, big data, and education. From 2016 to 2021, she was a Lecturer in Sleep Medicine at the Sleep and Circadian Neuroscience Institute, University of Oxford, training clinicians in the assessment, diagnosis, and treatment of sleep and circadian disorders. Prior to this appointment, Nicola was Associate Director of the Northumbria Centre for Sleep Research at Northumbria University, Newcastle upon Tyne, UK, from 2011 to 2016. In 2011, she completed her PhD at the University of London, focusing on Quantitative and Molecular Genetic Approaches to Understanding Sleep Quality and Diurnal Preference, for which she was awarded the Rising Researcher award in 2011. She received a first-class honours degree in Psychology from the University of Sussex.

LISTEN HERE:

https://sleep4performance.com/podcast/
s7-ep8-sleep-quality-phenotypes-chronotypes-
and-diurnal-preferences/

OR SCAN QR CODE

2.14 So, what if I still want to change between lark and owl?

Let's look at lark to owl. To change from lark to owl, you will need to increase the sleep opportunity in the morning. If you are aged 15-25, this should not be a large problem as there will be some hormonal drives towards a later bed and wake time to begin with. If you wake up early, try to stay in bed, keeping your bedroom as dark as possible. If you are hungry, have a small snack and return to bed. It is advised not to get out of bed until 8 am. You may wish to consider blocking natural light in your bedroom and using cooling with a fan or air conditioning. Staying in bed until this time may take several days or weeks to adapt. Remember that chronotype is an internal time clock many people cannot change significantly. However, those who try to change or go against the grain may experience a phenomenon known as social jet lag[26]. Social jet lag is a significant issue for shiftworkers and the population more broadly, with estimates from the World Health Organization (WHO) up to 300 million people.

2.15 Impact on alertness, performance, and productivity

Not achieving the recommended sleep (7-9 hrs) can impact your alertness. This impact may cause fluctuations in performance across the 24 hr day. In a research study of meter reading errors in Sweden across 20 years[36], indicates that errors are considerably more likely in the window of circadian low (03:00-06:00), with an additional slight increase in likelihood in the early afternoon (corresponding with the post-lunch dip or "siesta" time). These are the times when more attention needs to be paid when performing safety-critical tasks and should be considered when scheduling safety tasks.

Determining productivity impacts, variations, improvements, or losses for fatigue, sleepiness, and shiftwork is difficult. These measures will be different for all businesses. Let's say, for example, a business makes *"cement blocks"*. Trying to look for changes in production for a cement black factory that runs 24/7/365 may be difficult. The nature of work may vary in the demand for production and the number of people per shift. The first place to look if you want to see any change in productivity is hourly production rates and by hour.

Scientific insight: circadian rhythms and production

This is precisely what Simon Folkard and Philip Tucker [37] did when they analysed three studies looking at real-job measures of speed or accuracy over the 24 hr day. The measures they obtained were:

- delay in answering calls by switchboard operators

- errors in reading meters

- the time' spinners' took to tie broken threads in the textile industry

They averaged the data and generated a productivity score across the day, showing a time-of-day effect. What was evident is that there was (just like the study mentioned earlier) a significant reduction and variation in productivity between 22:00 and 06:00 and, after lunch, between 13:00 and 15:00.

This is similar to the trends we observe in biological rhythms, such as circadian rhythms, as described earlier. Similar findings in a study in Korea with more than 4,000 workers found that shiftworkers reduced productivity by 2.5%, and the most significant impact was the night shift. Those on the permanent night shift had 7.7% productivity losses compared to non-shift workers. These productivity losses were mainly attributable to absenteeism and productivity losses during shift work [38].

Sleep Disorders

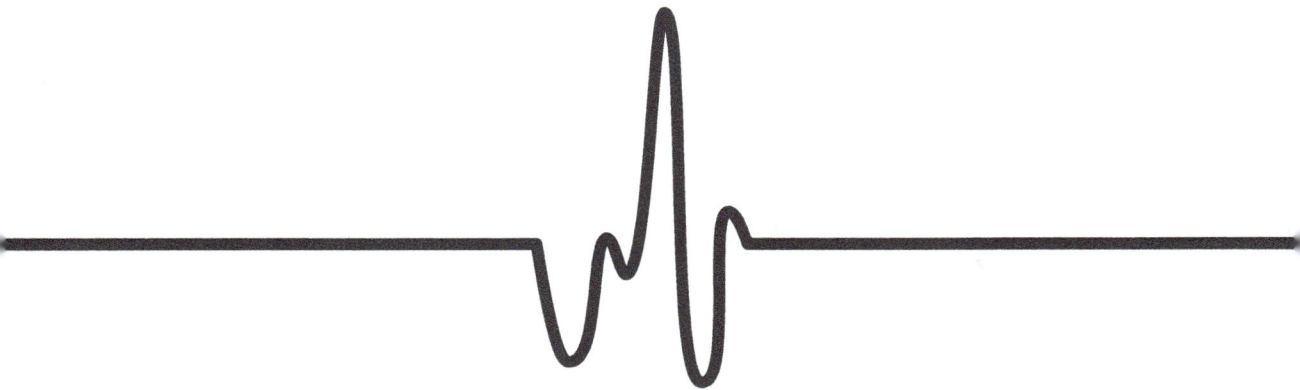

3. Sleep Disorders

3.1   What exactly are sleep disorders?

There are over 70 sleep disorders distributed amongst six categories within the International Classification of Sleep Disorders (ICSD- 3rd Ed)[39]. Categories include:

- Insomnia Disorders

- Sleep-Related Breathing Disorders

- Central Disorders of Hypersomnolence

- Circadian Rhythm Sleep-Wake Disorders

- Parasomnias

- Sleep-Related Movement Disorders

Sleep disorders affect approximately 22% of the Australian populatio[16]. Short-term effects can include a reduction in cognitive[40, 41] and physical performance[42], while long-term effects can include an increased risk of cardiovascular disease[43], diabetes[44] and testosterone reduction.

Sleep disorders affect many people and represent a significant safety risk in the workplace. The most common sleep disorders include obstructive sleep apnea (OSA), insomnia, shiftwork disorder (SWD), and periodic leg movement disorders (PLMs). Shiftwork disorder describes those who are not able to cope with working nights or rotating between different shifts and experience disturbed sleep and poor functioning while awake as a result. Sleep disorders can significantly impact work fitness and worsen the already detrimental impact of shiftwork fatigue risk factors (e.g., extended shifts, working during the night) described above.

Sleep disorders are some of the most common problems encountered in medical practices. In middle-aged adults, for example, 23% of women and 49% of men likely experience moderate to severe OSA[45]. Concerningly, the rate of sleep disorders has increased in the last two decades due to an aging and increasingly overweight population[46].

3.2 How are sleep disorders diagnosed?

For most sleep disorders (but not all), polysomnography (PSG) is the objective gold standard for measuring, monitoring, and assessing sleep in humans[47,48]. Typically, a PSG study is administered by a trained sleep technician. The American Academy of Sleep Medicine (AASM) describes the most widely accepted protocols. Brain, eye, and muscle activity are simultaneously measured using techniques called electroencephalography (EEG), electrooculography (EOG), and electromyography (EMG). Respiration (breathing) is monitored with nasal prongs, an oronasal thermistor (a small device between the nose and mouth), and thoracic and abdominal respiratory bands. Blood oxygen saturation (SaO_2) and heart rate are monitored continuously from a pulse oximeter (a small clip-like device) on the index finger. Leg movements are monitored by EMG electrodes placed over a lower leg muscle. Lastly, there is generally a position sensor, microphone and a live video feed (via an infrared camera monitor) set up within the room to detect body position and snoring[49].

The PSG examination of sleep provides a gold standard measurement of various sleep outcomes, including:

- Time in bed (TIB: the total time spent in bed, from lights out until time at wake)

- Total sleep time (TST: the number of minutes from the time of sleep onset to the last awakening, minus the number of minutes awake during this period)

- Sleep efficiency (SE: the total sleep time divided by time in bed, multiplied by 100)

- Sleep onset latency (SOL: the number of minutes from time at lights out to the time of sleep onset)

- Time awake after sleep onset (WASO; number of minutes awake, between the time of sleep onset and last awakening)

- Duration and percentage of time spent in different sleep stages

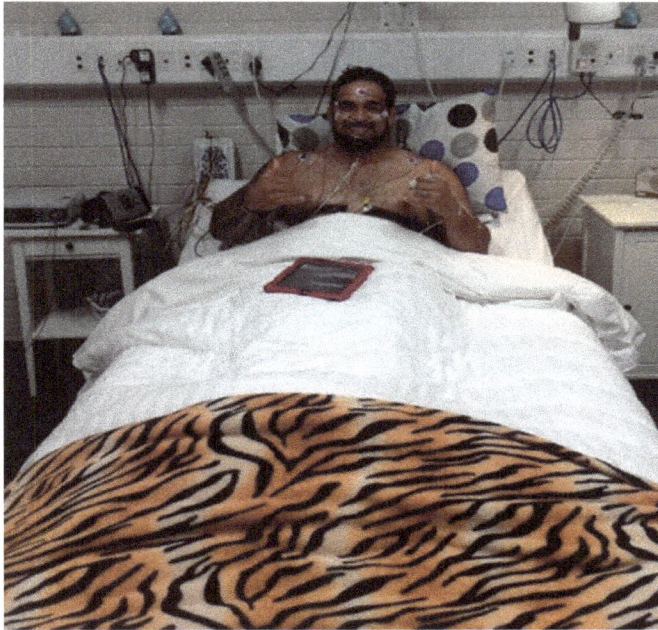

Figure 12. Super Rugby Athlete Undergoing an Overnight Polysomnography

3.3 What is the economic impact of sleep disorders?

Most sleep disorders are undiagnosed and thus remain untreated. In 2011, the Sleep Health Foundation in Australia commissioned Deloitte Economics to measure the indirect financial costs associated with sleep disorders in Australia. The results were astounding: each year, sleep disorders cost the Australian economy an estimated $4.3 billion due to: lost productivity ($3.1 billion), motor vehicle and workplace accidents ($646 million) and other costs ($472 million)[50]. Let's look at the more common sleep disorders in society today.

3.4   What is Obstructive Sleep Apnea (OSA)?

OSA is the most common sleep disorder in the general population, being experienced by more than 9% of Australian adults. OSA is characterised by the upper airway being either partially or completely obstructed (or collapsing), repeatedly throughout a night of sleep. This causes the brain to wake up, to increase the muscle tone of muscles involved in keeping the airway open. Once the brain is again receiving oxygen, the person falls asleep, the upper airway collapses or becomes obstructed again, and the person again wakes up. These collapses and accompanying wake episodes can happen more than 30 times per hr in severe cases. Modifiable factors that may increase OSA risk include:

- Obesity

- Alcohol

- Smoking

- Medications

- Sleeping position (Lying on your back)

Studies investigating risk factors in the general population have shown that neck circumference (>42 cm) and Body Mass Index (BMI) are good predictors of the severity of OSA. Other factors that are not easily modifiable include:

- Craniofacial features (jaw shape)

- Ethnicity

- Biological sex

- Age

- Pregnancy

Obstructive sleep apnea is strongly associated with adverse health outcomes, including cardiovascular disease[51] and diabetes[52]. If untreated, OSA can result in poorer performance[53] and an increased risk of a motor vehicle crash or other workplace accidents/injuries[54,55].

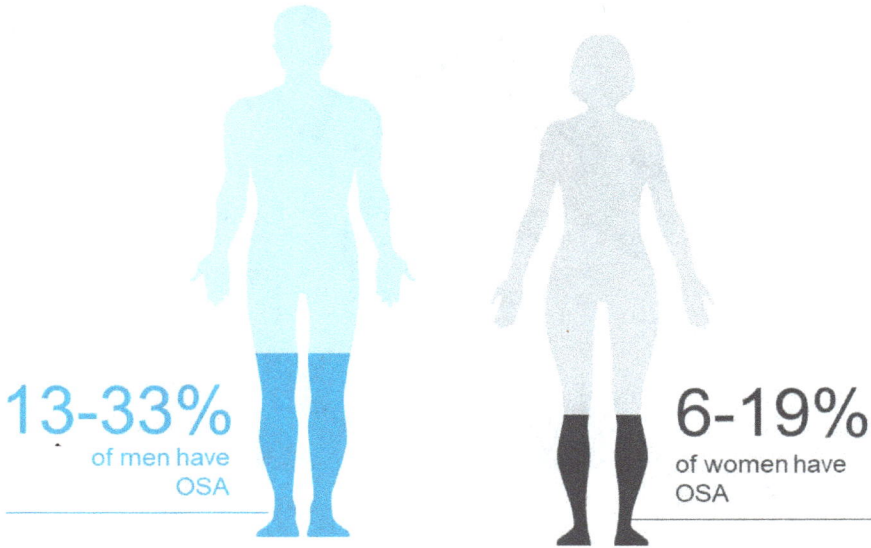

13-33%
of men have
OSA

6-19%
of women have
OSA

Figure 13. OSA Prevalence in Males and Females [56]

Scientific insight: prevalence of OSA and body weight

In a study looking at nearly five thousand police officers in the United States of America (USA), it was found that 40% screened positive for at least one sleep disorder, of which 34% were positive for OSA [57]. Another study with over 1 million participants found that participants with a Body Mass Index (BMI) greater than 40 kg/m^2 are over 27 times more likely to have OSA [58], compared to those of healthy weight.

3.5 What are the treatment options for OSA?

For those who may be diagnosed with OSA, there are a range of treatment options. These may include:

- **Continuous Positive Airway Pressure,** better known as CPAP. Essentially, this blows oxygen into your airway whilst you sleep (pneumatic splint) to keep it open and can reduce sleep apnea episodes by >90%

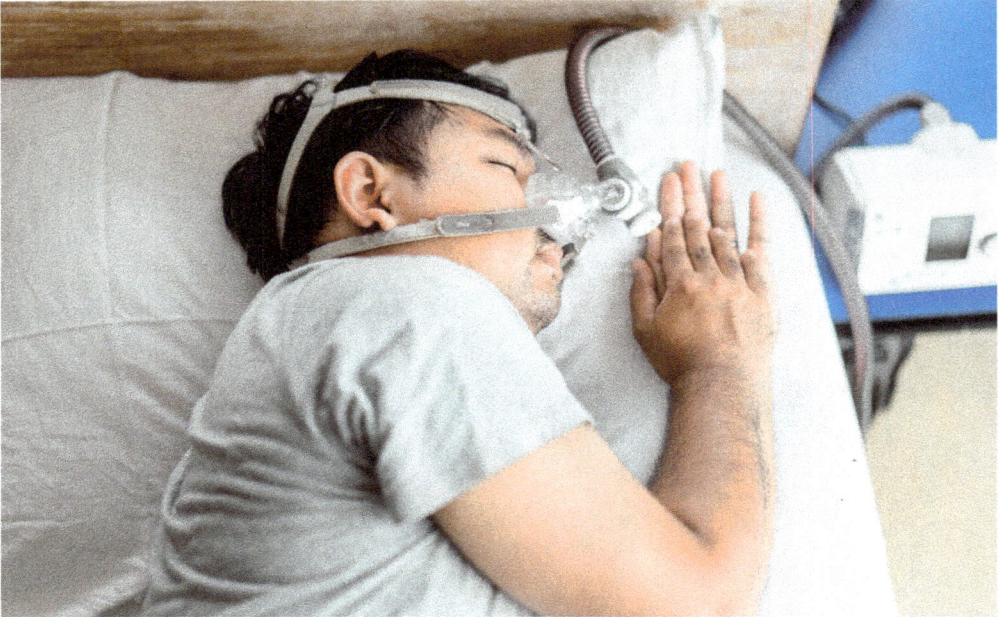

Figure 14. CPAP Treatment

- There are also **mandibular advancement splints (MAS).** These are often used when people cannot tolerate CPAP or for those with milder OSA. MAS holds the tongue and mandible forward to help the person breathe (mechanical splint)

- **Positional therapy:** some people only have OSA events when they are lying on their back. Therefore, if someone is taught to sleep on their side, the episodes can reduce significantly for OSA

- **Reduction of body weight,** reducing one's body weight to a BMI of <30kgm[2] is beneficial and can eliminate OSA in most people. There is evidence of sleep quality improving and OSA symptoms reducing for those with OSA after undertaking regular aerobic exercise [59]

- In rare cases, **surgery** may be required to ensure an airway can be maintained. Surgeries may include nasal, oropharynx, tongue, jawbone and more [60]

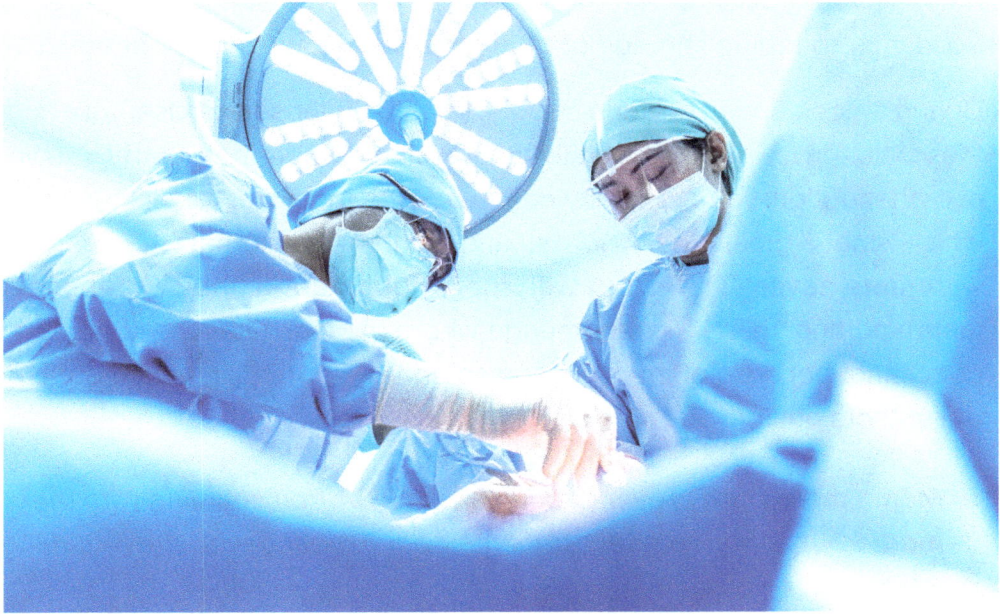

Figure 15. Surgical Treatment for Sleep Disorders

3.6   Is mouth taping an effective treatment for OSA?

Mouth taping is a popular trend on TikTok and other social media outlets. According to social media posts about it, it alleviates some of the negative effects of mouth breathing, such as snoring and dry mouth. Mouth breathing at night has also been linked to developmental and behavioural problems in children and an increased risk of OSA. The proposed manner of how mouth taping stops mouth breathing is simple: if your mouth is taped shut, you cannot breathe with your mouth open while you sleep, hopefully forcing you to breathe through your nose instead.

Only one pilot study was performed on mouth taping over eight years ago, finding benefits for participants with mild OSA[61]. However, in this study, all participants were checked to see if they had an adequate nasal airway for nose breathing before participating. This raises an important question: if mouth breathing contributes to your OSA, why are you mouth breathing in the first place? A blockage of nasal airways commonly causes mouth breathing. If this is the cause, obviously taping your mouth closed is a terrible idea. Some products specifically designed for mouth taping do not limit your ability to breathe; if these specially designed products are used, mouth taping should not be dangerous. However, is it beneficial?

During a sleep apnea episode and just like after intense exercise, your body tries to take in oxygen through the faster available route: the mouth. By taping over that option, you are depriving the body of the fastest available option, which is not a great idea. Also, Jau and friends [62] found that when patients with more severe OSA slept with their mouth taped, they experienced mouth puffing: this is a phenomenon where the individual tries to breathe but cannot because of the tape, and so ends up puffing in their mouth. As the authors put it,

> *"Mouth taping can prevent patients with OSA from inhaling with the mouth but cannot prevent patients from exhaling with the mouth."*

Given how little scientific evidence there is for mouth taping (one pilot study from over eight years ago, which has not been replicated) and due to a good nasal airway being a necessity, we do not recommend using mouth taping for OSA or sleep more generally. Reducing body weight (particularly for the 41% of people with OSA who are also overweight or obese [63]), avoiding alcohol before bedtime, avoiding sleep medications and avoiding sleeping on your back are all far better first steps to take for OSA. At the same time, CPAP and MAS are treatment methods with much greater demonstrated effectiveness than mouth taping.

3.7   Is snoring a sleep disorder?

While snoring is not a classified sleep disorder, it can cause sleep problems for bed partners. Snoring is a common condition, affecting approximately 35% of adults and is twice as common in men. Snoring is defined as turbulent airflow vibrating upper airway soft tissues in the nasal passage (nose) and throat. Snoring is more common:

- Following alcohol ingestion

- When lying on your back

- In sleep-deprived individuals

Significantly, if an individual snores, this does not mean they have sleep apnea. However, individuals who have sleep apnea almost always snore.

Snoring can impact the bed partner more than the person. For the bed partner, the first place to address this is the location. If you have a spare room or can sleep in a different part of the house, you should do so. You do not want your sleep and next day functioning to be impacted by snoring if you can help it. Secondly, you should talk to your partner about the problem. An honest conversation and an explanation of why you are choosing to sleep in a separate room will likely put far less strain on your relationship than baring through the snoring and being persistently tired (and likely grumpy!) during the day.

You should also encourage the snoring partner to go to the General Practitioner (GP) get a referral to a sleep physician and address their snoring. It may or may not be due to an underlying sleep disorder such as OSA. Still, it should be investigated to get to the root of the cause and ultimately resolve or mitigate the problem. Snoring can be challenging to manage and addressing it can potentially stress a relationship. Still, it is incredibly important to be mindful of your sleep and daytime functioning and address a bed partner's snoring.

3.8   What is insomnia?

Each night, we jump into bed, tired and weary from the day, and consciously fall asleep. However, many of us struggle to fall or stay asleep. Our minds often start racing, thoughts and problems from the day begin to emerge, and the problems seem to compound, leading to stress, anxiety, and difficulty relaxing.

Insomnia can be defined as an inability to fall asleep or remain asleep for an adequate length of time.

Short periods of insomnia (acute insomnia), which may be related to stress or a significant life event (i.e., grief from the loss of a loved one), are common and generally not a long-term concern. Acute insomnia may also be caused by changes to work schedules, such as shiftwork or travel across time zones, resulting in jet lag. However, insomnia may also be experienced on a long-term basis (chronic insomnia). Recent data reports that insomnia may be experienced by up to 30% of people[64]. Left untreated, insomnia can cause social and psychological issues and can lead to poor performance in the workplace.

Insomnia is categorised into three types.

- **Sleep onset insomnia** – I can't get to sleep at night

- **Sleep maintenance insomnia** – I can't stay asleep at night

- **Early morning awakening insomnia**. – I always wake up earlier than I want

Insomnia can be further segregated into two additional categories:

- **Primary insomnia** is defined as sleeplessness that cannot be attributed to a medical, psychological, or environmental cause. In other words, no other contributing factors exist

- **Secondary insomnia** is sleeplessness that can be attributed directly to another condition or cause

Insomnia is associated with many negative physical health outcomes, such as hypertension[65] and cardiovascular disease[66], as well as mental health outcomes, including depression, anxiety, bipolar disorders and suicidal ideation[67].

Insomnia can also lead to impaired cognitive functioning[68] and reduced workplace productivity[69], ultimately reducing fitness for work. Both diagnosing and treating insomnia can be challenging. For a clinical diagnosis of insomnia, one must have difficulty falling or staying asleep for

1. At least 30 mins a night

2. Three or more nights per week

3. Experience an impact to daytime functioning whereby you feel sleepy and less alert during the day

To be considered chronic insomnia, these difficulties must persist for three months or more. The diagnosis of insomnia is not conducted within a laboratory setting; an overnight PSG will not help identify the prevalence of insomnia. Instead, an insomnia diagnosis requires using actigraphy (a wearable sleep monitoring device) and a sleep diary. However, before looking towards an insomnia diagnosis, you should consider the following:

3.9 Strategies to reduce stress and anxiety before bedtime.

- **Plan for tomorrow, today**: Creating a plan in the evening for the following day and ensuring that the following day's work schedule is set can be a great first step. This can help get the next day's worries out of your head and onto paper, reducing the stress of forgetting an important task or an exciting idea you may have thought of

- **Schedule some worry time in the evening**: Scheduling time in the evening (ideally >30 mins before bedtime) where you allow yourself to worry may prevent these same worries from creeping into your mind come bedtime. Alternatively, you can try a daily review. This could be as simple as:

  - What went well today?

  - What didn't go so well today?

  - What am I going to do tomorrow to improve?

- **Switch off and avoid work**, including emails, for at least 1 hr before bed. This will drastically reduce stress, promoting the transition into slumber

- **Distraction through mindfulness-based apps, meditations, music and podcasts** may also help. However, using distractions that are not stimulating or stressful is important. Listening to or watching the latest news headlines or the financial outlook may not be the best. Additionally, scrolling through social media shortly before bed (bedtime procrastination) is not ideal for many reasons, including not being able to control what you see next (the next post you see could simulate or stress you out!), and that these media outlets use algorithms which promote media that will specifically stimulate you and keep you engaged

For many people, addressing sleep hygiene can reduce the impact of insomnia. Some important changes or considerations include:

- Limiting or eliminating naps, especially late in the day
- Restricting alcohol, caffeine, and tobacco products in the evening
- Avoiding late-night meals (particularly large meals within 1 hr of bedtime)
- Limiting screentime before bedtime
- Avoiding work, video games, and other stimulating activities in bed (and in the bedroom, if feasible)
- Maintaining a healthy diet
- Exercising regularly during the day
- Following a consistent sleep schedule
- Using the bedroom only for sleep and sex

3.10 What is Cognitive Behavior Therapy for Insomnia (CBT-I)?

CBT-I is the recommended treatment for those who still experience insomnia despite trying the above treatments. CBT-I involves working with a qualified therapist (although online/ telehealth CBT-I treatments are gaining traction) to change thinking patterns about sleep. Expert contributors to the Australian Government's inquiry into sleep health described CBT-I as containing the following components[70].

- Sleep psychoeducation (understanding normal sleep and its determinants)
- Sleep hygiene (environmental and lifestyle factors that may affect sleep)
- Sleep restriction therapy
- Stimulus control therapy
- Relaxation training

- Cognitive therapy (dealing with dysfunctional thoughts and attitudes about sleep)

- Mindfulness therapy

Regarding relaxation training, we note that practising yoga, relaxation techniques, meditation, tai-chi, relaxing music, breathing techniques, and cognitive relaxation have been reported to increase sleep duration and reduce insomnia symptoms.

Guided Meditation to promote sleep with Alexis Santos

Alexis graduated from Harvard University in 1995 and has been in the field of mindfulness and meditation since 2001. It was while travelling in India that he was introduced to insight meditation. Alexis has practised in many meditative styles and traditions, including with Sayadaw U Tejaniya, the Thai Forest tradition with Ajahn Sumedho, the Tibetan tradition with Yongey Mingyur Rinpoche and within the lay Western insight community where he continues to learn from the growing diversity of voices. Alexis teaches meditation at retreat centres around the world. He brings a practical, intuitive and compassionate approach to the development of wisdom.

LISTEN HERE:

https://youtu.be/
a6tyshS3akM?si=0tzwKB08iX-ODXy1

OR SCAN QR CODE

Want to know more about insomnia, CBT-I and mindfulness **?**

Season 2 Episode 6: Sleep and Mindfulness With special guest: Dr Melissa J Ree, Clinical Psychologist, BSc (Hons) MPsych (Clinical) PhD. Melissa completed a master's degree in clinical psychology and a PhD with distinction at the University of Western Australia in 2001. After her PhD Melissa worked at the University of Oxford as a Postdoctoral Research Fellow in the Department of Psychiatry. Since returning to Perth, Melissa has continued to be active in treatment, training, and research into psychological aspects of insomnia, anxiety, and depression. Melissa works in both clinical and research roles at private psychiatric hospitals in Perth and has been in private practice since 2004.

LISTEN HERE:

https://sleep4performance.com/podcast/
dr-melissa-ree-sleep-and-mindfulness/

OR SCAN QR CODE

3.11 What is shift work disorder (SWD)?

SWD can affect around 27% of shift workers[71]. It has been associated with sleep-related accidents, absenteeism, depression, and disruption to family and social life[72]. Shift work disorder causes difficulties adjusting to a different sleep/wake routine due to the circadian variation people experience working day, evening, or night shifts[71].

Diagnosis of SWD can be difficult and requires a similar approach to that of insomnia. Individuals with SWD very often also have another sleep disorder present, which is unsurprising given that shift workers have higher rates (compared to non-shift workers) of suffering from excessive daytime sleepiness, insomnia, and limb movement sleep disorders.

Some other sleep disorders that people may experience include:

- **Narcolepsy:** Narcolepsy is a sudden and overwhelming desire to sleep (often referred to as a sleep attack), which is usually accompanied by cataplexy (a sudden loss of muscle tone) and is often triggered by excitement[73]

- **Periodic Leg Movement Disorders (PLM)** are unusual leg movements that affect sleep by causing disruptions and lowering sleep duration and quality. In the general population, the prevalence rates of PLMs are 4%. Iron depletion may exacerbate PLM. Depending on the physical activity during the day, administering iron supplementation may benefit the treatment. Similar to PLM is restless leg syndrome (RLS), where the individual has an uncontrollable urge to move their legs while sitting still or lying down. PLM and RLS often come together; if someone has RLS, they are much more likely to have PLM

- **Sleep talking and walking, sleep terrors & sleep paralysis**. These disorders have been found to occur in the transition between sleep stages, for example, between REM and NREM sleep or when the brain is transitioning between sleep and wake. Parasomnias are more common in children and young adults [74]

Want to know more about sleep disorders? ?

Special Series on Sleep Disorders, Sleep4Performance Podcast, Special Series Sleep Disorders and Problems with Brendan Duffy. The legend of Long Island, USA, Mr Brendan Duffy. With a special interest in the realm of sports and fatigue management. Brendan Duffy has over 20 years of sleep medicine experience as a sleep tech and a sleep centre manager. He speaks, and authors articles nationally on the impact of sleep on athletic competition and preparation. He is a Registered Polysomnography Technician and a New York state-licensed sleep technologist and educator. In addition, he has spoken at several community and industry sleep meetings on several sleep topics. He is particularly interested in research and information regarding sleep and athletic performance. In this episode, Brendan gives us an excellent overview of how we have progressed in measuring sleep over time and retells some great stories. Check it out at:

LISTEN HERE:

https://sleep4performance.com/podcast/
ss-ep01-sleep-disorders-and-problems/

OR SCAN QR CODE

Want to know more about sleep medicine? ?

Season 3 Episode 11: The Sleep Physician with Dr David Cunnington: A specialist sleep physician who delivers healthcare to individuals with complex sleep problems and promotes sleep health through education. He is the co-director of Melbourne Sleep Disorders Centre, a multidisciplinary sleep clinic for diagnosing and treating sleep disorders.

David undertook sleep medicine training in Australia and Boston at Harvard Medical School. In addition to sleep medicine training, David has international qualifications in behavioural sleep medicine, using non-drug treatments to manage sleep. David regularly appears in print, radio, and TV media as an expert commentator on sleep.

In this episode, we discuss David's inspirations, studies, and international work, along with current research, new technologies, and future advancements in sleep measurement. You can check out SleepHub, where David and his partner Kris provide information on all things sleep, including trending topics, tools and tips, the Sleep Talk Podcast, and much more.

LISTEN HERE:

https://sleep4performance.com/podcast/
s3-ep011-the-sleep-physician/

OR SCAN QR CODE

- **For people with REM behaviour disorder:** During REM sleep, the body completely paralyses almost all of its muscles as a defence mechanism to stop you from playing out your dreams (recall from section 1 that ~80% of dreams occur during REM sleep). REM Behaviour Disorder (RBD), this paralysis or muscle atonia ceases to work. This can cause an individual to shout, talk, sing, or even swear while asleep. RBD is present in 20% of people incurring a head injury due to an incident[75]

- **Bruxism** is a common condition characterised by the grinding or clenching of teeth, often during sleep. Bruxism can result in several problems, including sleep disruption, headaches, jaw pain, tooth wear and fractures. Stress and anxiety are frequently linked to bruxism, although its exact causes can vary. Approximately 15% of adults have bruxism. However, this number does decrease with age[76]

Sleep Loss, Performance and Shiftwork

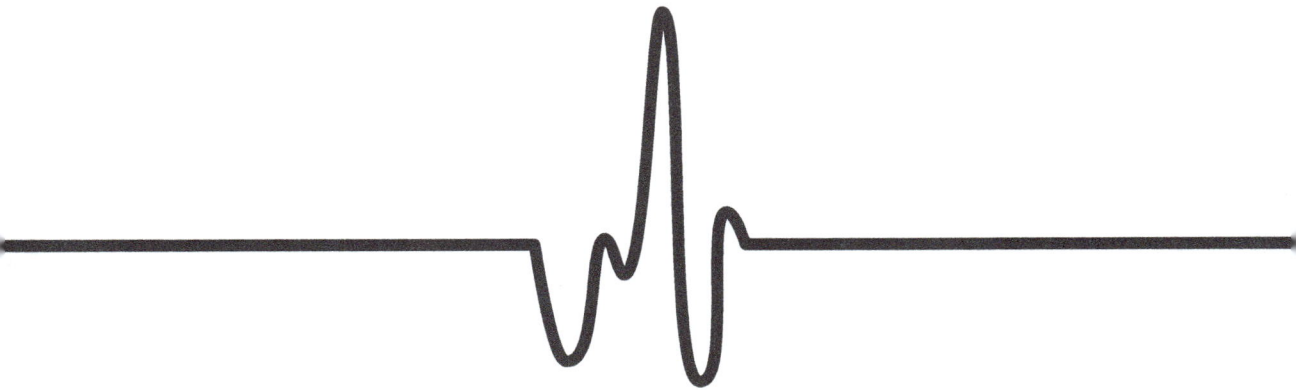

4. Sleep Loss, Performance and Shiftwork

4.1   What is fatigue?

Many people use the word fatigue to describe how they feel from the adverse effects of sleep loss, restriction, or deprivation that they may have experienced. Fatigue may be characterised as an impaired ability to function or perform in terms of physical, mental, or emotional performance (or a combination of the three!). It can affect anyone, and most (if not all) adults will experience fatigue at some point.

Each year, around 2 million Australians see their doctor about fatigue. This may be due to working shiftwork, extended work hours or the intensity of the work such as seasonal work, construction projects or intensive military operations, to name a few. However, when we look at the broader definition of fatigue, it may include or be related to additional factors, such as

- Physical exertion

- Lack of physical fitness

- Excess bodyweight (overweight or obesity)

- Emotional stress or grief

- Boredom

- Regular alcohol use

- Poor diet

- Medication

- Autoimmune disorders

- Sleep disorders

- Mental health issues, such as depression and anxiety

Shift workers and those who work irregular hours are more susceptible to experiencing fatigue from sleep loss (compared to non-shift workers) as they often experience sleep loss due to difficulty getting adequate sleep when sleep patterns change. Sleep loss and disruption to sleep and wake behaviours are common among shift workers. Sleep loss leading to fatigue may result in the following signs (what you will see in yourself and others) and symptoms (what you or others may feel).

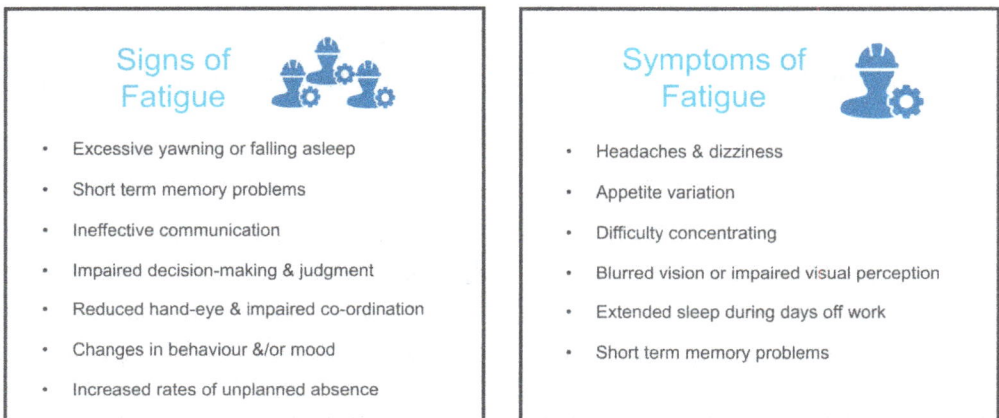

Signs of Fatigue	Symptoms of Fatigue
• Excessive yawning or falling asleep	• Headaches & dizziness
• Short term memory problems	• Appetite variation
• Ineffective communication	• Difficulty concentrating
• Impaired decision-making & judgment	• Blurred vision or impaired visual perception
• Reduced hand-eye & impaired co-ordination	• Extended sleep during days off work
• Changes in behaviour &/or mood	• Short term memory problems
• Increased rates of unplanned absence	

Figure 16. Signs and Symptoms of Fatigue

4.2   Sleep loss, performance and the relationship with alcohol

You may have previously heard comparisons between a lack of sleep and being legally drunk or comparisons to blood alcohol concentrations (BAC). This comparison is not made because we behave like we are intoxicated or stumble around when sleep-deprived; it is made because our reaction times degrade in a similar manner to when we are drunk.

Scientific insight: the impact of sleep loss on day-to-day performance

In a landmark study[6], 48 healthy participants were kept in a laboratory for up to 14 days and nights. They were divided into four groups, with 12 people in each group. These groups were

Group 1: Maximum of 8 hrs of sleep opportunity allowed per night

Group 2: Maximum of 6 hrs of sleep opportunity allowed per night

Group 3: Maximum of 4 hrs of sleep opportunity allowed per night

Group 4: No sleep opportunity allowed (this group stopped at 3 days)

The research team found a significant increase in reaction times and a decrease in vigilance across the 14 days, with lower amounts of sleep opportunity resulting in poorer performance. The results from the study suggest that performance after 9-10 nights with only 6 hrs of sleep is similar to performance following a single night of total sleep deprivation (24 hrs without sleep). Furthermore, performance after 9-10 nights with only 4 hrs of sleep is similar to 2 full nights of total sleep deprivation (48 hrs without sleep). This study highlights that cumulative or consecutive nights of low sleep significantly affect performance and reinforces that getting enough sleep regularly is important for performance and functioning.

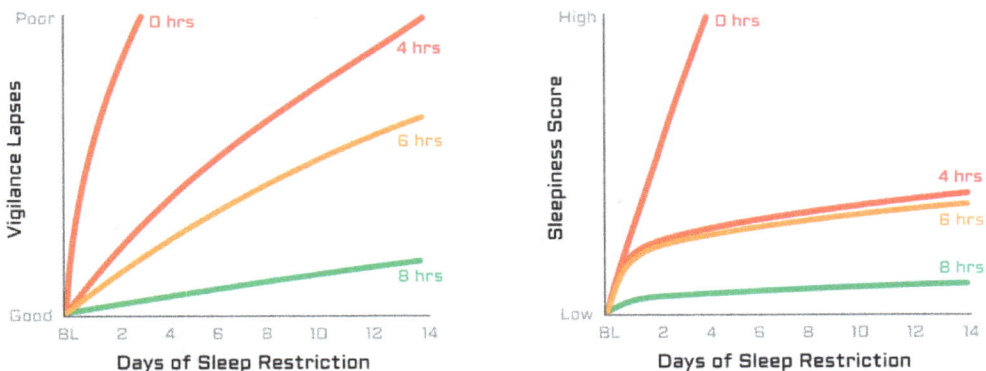

Figure 17 Sleep Restriction and Performance and Self-Reported Sleepiness

Scientific insight: hours of awake and blood alcohol concentrate

These comparisons are made primarily using the research results conducted by Drew Dawson and Nicole Lamond[77]. In this study, 22 healthy young adults consumed alcoholic beverages until their BAC reached 0.10%, while simultaneously being tested on a motor tracking task every 30 mins; as expected, performance declined with increasing BAC. On a separate day, participants were again tested on the same test every 30 mins, this time without alcohol, but for consecutive hours without sleep. After 17 hrs, performance quickly declined, and after 19 hrs, performance was equivalent to that at a BAC of 0.05%. Other studies have shown that performance after 17 hrs awake is similar to that with a BAC of 0.05%. Practically, this suggests that if you wake up at 06:00 and are still awake (perhaps driving) at 23:00, you will have a reaction time similar to a BAC of 0.05%.

Want to know more about sleep and alcohol?

Season 7 Episode 10: Sleep, Shiftwork, Alcohol, and more with Professor Jill Dorrian. Jill is a Professor in Psychology with a PhD in sleep and chronobiology research and a Master of Biostatistics. From the beginning of her PhD, Jill conducted laboratory and field studies with a consistent focus on collaboration and translation. The Australian Shiftwork and Workload Consortium, a 10-year collaboration with Australian Rail Industry operators and safety regulators, supported her PhD and early post-doctoral work. This work informed rail fatigue risk management (the over-arching term to describe risks relating to sleep loss and performance impairment in the industry).

LISTEN HERE:

https://sleep4performance.podbean.com/e/season-7-episode-10-w-prof-jill-dorrian-the-dean-who-is-not-mean-average-on-sleep-shiftwork-alcohol-and-lots-more/

OR SCAN QR CODE

4.3   What is shiftwork?

Shiftwork refers to any work schedule that extends beyond the typical *"9-to-5"* workday. With an increased need for flexibility in the modern workplace, work hours can be scheduled for up to 24 hrs a day, seven days a week. Sleep loss and fatigue are inevitable consequences of a *"round-the-clock operation",* so fatigue-risk management is essential to safe work practice. Beyond the immediate effects of fatigue, shift work can result in adverse health outcomes, decreased quality of life, and an increased likelihood of family problems, including divorce rates.

Today, most people are most likely in some form of shiftwork with flexible work arrangements, remote work, and hybrid approaches; the standard *"9-to-5"* workday is slowly fading. The ability to stay connected with technology, thereby, the ability to work, means that many of us may never have a standard workday.

There are several types of shift work. In general, we refer to the following types:

- **Permanent or fixed shift work:** You are assigned to a specific shift type (e.g., days, evenings, nights), and you continuously work on this system. A classic example of a permanent shift worker is your local baker; bakers work very early morning hours, such as 04:00-12:00 (midday)

- **Rotating schedule shift work:** You rotate from days to evenings, then nights, or backwards from nights to evenings, then day shift. Many individuals in the mining industry or factories are rotating schedule shift workers

- **Irregular:** You may work a fixed or rotating schedule, but it may change occasionally, or you may be a casual or relief worker and work no fixed schedule. An example of an irregular shift worker could be a student who works one or two nights a week in a bar or pub

When looking at shiftwork, a range of questions may arise, such as

- What is the best shift length?

- When should I start and finish?

- How many days or nights can I work?

- What if I work in mining and fly in and out?

- What if I work on construction projects?

The following answers may be beneficial.

4.4   What is the best time to start a work shift?

Consideration of shift timing is a crucial factor when devising a roster. Hours of the day are not uniform. While conventional shifts include day, afternoon, evening shifts, or night shifts, today, various organisations implement systems starting outside these traditional periods. It's essential to account for shift duration when addressing shift start times. Generally, eight-hour shifts follow these start times:

- Day shifts typically begin between 06:00-08:00

- Afternoon/evening shifts typically begin between 14:00-16:00

- Night shifts usually start between 22:00-0:00

For organisations employing 12 hr shifts, the typical start times are:

- Day shifts typically begin between 05:00-08:00

- Night shifts usually begin between 17:00-20:00

To add further complexity, factors such as employee preferences, location, commute to work location, ambient heat of the work environment, labour laws in that region, and the specific chronotype of the individual doing the shift may all factor into decisions around shift start times. Larks prefer early morning shift start times, whereas owls prefer a later start time for day and night shifts. However, it is crucial to balance these preferences and practicalities. One important practicality is the commute duration to the workplace. Some workers may commute for an hour or more each way for a 10-12 hr shift. Commuting time may exacerbate the shift timing and duration risk, mainly when daily commutes are of this length.

Scientific insight: impact of start times in a fly-in, fly-out mining operation

A study in the Western Australian mining industry, with fly-in and fly-out workers [78] living in a remote camp for up to two weeks, found that the shift start time significantly impacted the amount of sleep mining shift workers obtained. In this remote fly-in fly-out mine site, shiftworkers started their 12.5 hr work shift at 05:30. However, to be present for the start of the shift, they had to wake up at 04:00 to shower, eat breakfast, and pack their lunch and snacks for the day before departing on a 20 min commute via bus to the mining operation. The cumulative time of the work shift and these other preparatory activities left little time for other important tasks, such as exercise, relaxation, contacting family, and sleep, often meaning that workers were not achieving a 7–9 hr sleep window.

For day shifts, the earlier they start (particularly before 06:00 am), the more likely sleep opportunity will be reduced. Importantly, by missing out on sleep at the end of the night, we deprive ourselves of periods of REM sleep, which happen more frequently in the latter half of the night between 03:00 and 06:00. Losing out on REM sleep may result in daytime sleepiness and the urge to sleep, difficulty in concentrating, and poor memory recall.

With night shifts, the primary consideration lies (no pun intended) not in the start time but rather in the finish time. The start of night shifts generally coincides with the forbidden zone or the wake maintenance zone (approximately 18:00-21:00). At this time, alertness tends to be high, and sleepiness tends to be low [27]. The same cannot be said about the end hours of typical night shifts. The end of 12 hr night shifts often coincides with the window of circadian low (WOCL; between 03:00-06:00), whereby there is naturally a reduction in alertness and focus. A phenomenon known as the second wind or a surge of energy coinciding with the sunrise (considering the significant role light plays) may be experienced due to circadian rhythm mechanisms, but this second wind is short-lived. For example, if driving during this period or when returning home and deciding to drive children to school, this situation poses a potential risk.

Scientific insight: changing shift timing to reduce accident risk

One research group aimed to do something entirely different to combat these risks. Recognising that the Window of Circadian Low is most pronounced between 03:00 and 06:00 [79], collaborating with an underground mining operation, restructured their shifts and roster system. The critical adjustment ensured no one was scheduled to work during the critical 03:00-06:00 period. The trial involved implementing 2x10 hr shifts (day shift from 07:00 to 17:00, night shift from 17:00 to 03:00).

Although this reduced operational uptime by approximately 4 hrs, it significantly lowered hours lost due to accidental injuries at the site from 4400 to 2206 hrs (~50% reduction). This case underscores the advantages of eliminating work during these early morning hours or minimising the workforce during this timeframe. Furthermore, it emphasises the benefit of avoiding high-risk or safety-critical tasks between 03:00-06:00. If essential business operations occur during this time, appropriate controls, including a thorough risk assessment, should be implemented.

4.5   What is the difference between the shift length of 8 hrs, 10 hrs or 12 hrs?

Many people ask this question, assuming that the shorter the shift duration, the lower the risk for sleep loss resulting in fatigue. Shiftworkers may have different preferences concerning working hours, depending on how it impacts their time off, frequency of shifts, or pay. This question may be answered from a human resource, safety, health, financial, operations or employee perspective, highlighting the difficulty and complexity of developing, deploying, and working in a shift and roster system. When we consider the shift length independent of any other factors, we may wish to think about the following:

Frequency: If a person undertakes 8 hr shifts, they will be required to go to and from work at least five times a week to achieve a 40 hr week.

Conversely, a 10 hr shift will need a person to go to and from work four times a week to achieve a 40 hr week, and a 12 hr shift will require a person to go to work three to four times a week. Shiftworkers may prefer to maximise shift length to reduce shifts frequency. This, in turn, allows more days off to rest and recover or spend time with family. In addition, it may reduce the cost of commuting to and from the workplace, as this is required for fewer shifts.

Work type: The type of work performed within a shift must be considered, including physical workload, cognitive demands, safety-critical tasks, environmental factors such as heat and humidity, and the nature of the workspace, such as working with heights or confined spaces.

Resources: Shift durations (8, 10, 12 hrs) can impact the resources required, such as the workers or leaders required, equipment, transport and accommodation facilities (particularly for fly-in fly-out operations).

Costs: How does this impact pay or salary if the workforce wishes to move to an 8, 10 or 12 hr shift system? Many shiftworkers on a 12 hr shift and roster system ask to move back to an 8 hr shift system; however, when the financial impacts of a roster change are discussed, many prefer to stay on a 12 hr shift system.

4.6 Practical application for designing shifts and roster systems

- When designing a shift system, the type of activity during work hours and whether the tasks are safety-critical must be considered

- Consultation with the workforce must address employee preferences and local requirements

- Management should consider a shift and roster system's impact on people, production, and the financial implications (wages, salaries, and costs) during its development

- If a 12 hr shift system is used, consideration must be given to the frequency of breaks within a shift and the opportunity to eat, hydrate, and rest

- Avoid early morning starts before 06:00, where possible

- Consider workers' preparation time and commute time before the commencement of a shift

- Avoid high-risk work between 03:00-06:00 as it can significantly increase incidents and accidents

- Avoid finishing night shifts after 07:00 to minimise risk when commuting home

- Utilise experts to assist in developing shifts and roster patterns with biomathematical modelling to reduce organisational risk and limit employee exposure

- For shiftworkers, avoid or minimise your exposure to night shifts and ensure you maintain a healthy lifestyle to protect yourselves against the impact of shiftwork

- In general, designing a shift and roster system that is forward rotating is best (Days to Nights)

- Backward rotating rosters (Nights to Days) may lead to more incidents, injuries, and social, health, and business impacts?

- Consider the workforce's age, demographic and choices if you are designing a shift and roster system

Scientific insight: the risk associated with hours of work

There is still much research to be done to understand risk factors within the shiftwork arena; we know that time on task or time at work comes with increased risk. The impact of time on task has been well discussed, including in a review paper by Folkard and Tucker [37]. In this review, Folkard and Tucker report that relative risk increased by type of shift: day (lowest), evening and night shift (highest risk), with an increase in risk when the shift went beyond 10 hrs. Another interesting finding reported in this review is that risk increases within a shift as a function of time spent since the last break within the shift.

In an applied study by Lowden and friends in a chemical plant [80], they assessed moving from a rotating 3-shift (8 hr) to a 2-shift shift (12 hr) with control room operators; the study found that shift change increased satisfaction with work hours, sleep, and time for social activities, resulted in an improvement in alertness and recovery time after night shift decreased. This may be due to fewer shift changes and shifts, resulting in more time off. However, when changing from an 8 hr work period to a 12 hr work period, some factors may lead to insufficient rest and sleep opportunities between shifts; these include other jobs, courses, education or businesses workers are participating in or developing, or other hobbies/ activities.

4.7 Why do companies make us work the night shift if it's risky?

The main reasons a company requires a night shift are to maximise productivity, generate a return on investment or assets, and reduce cost, particularly in large asset-based organisations such as mining, oil and gas, and manufacturing, to name a few. In addition, there may be a requirement to work night shifts in particular industries such as airlines, air traffic control, rail operations, power and water, or other utilities. Many companies may have global operations, requiring support to be available 24/7.

It is important to note that such companies do not enforce night shift work; it is a condition of employment or part of the employment that people volunteer to sign up for and should be part of the contract offered to you. If you do not wish to work the night shift, you should not apply for jobs requiring night shift work. However, companies with workers undertaking night shifts should try to minimise the risk of night shift work through several means, such as education training, occupational health systems, promotion of regular breaks, and fatigue leader checklists.

4.8 Is it better to work a permanent night shift?

Many people report that when they work permanent night shift, they feel better or adapt to it over time. While some have argued that permanent night work may have benefits in terms of circadian adjustment to shift work, the scientific consensus is that permanent night shift work is not a good idea. Lots of epidemiology research has looked at this idea over the years. This research has found that permanent night shift work increases the odds of developing cancer. It is also important to remember that humans are diurnal animals[81]; we are meant to be awake during the day and asleep during the night. We are not designed to work on a permanent night shift roster and can never fully adapt to the night shift[82].

There is little support for this argument that we can fully adjust to a permanent night shift schedule, according to field experts Torbjörn Åkerstedt and Kenneth Wright[83]. For all people working at night, night work is the most significant contributing factor to poor alertness and wakefulness, resulting in fatigue. This increases accident risk and injury[37, 84,85]. This is due to night shift workers attempting to sleep during the day when the internal biological clock is promoting wake while trying to stay awake and work when the internal biological clock is promoting *sleep.*

A review of shift work risk reports that accident risk increases by 30% on the night shift compared to working during the day[84]. Similar findings have been reported in other studies with injury and accident risk increase on night shifts compared to day shifts 86.[86]. In addition, the more night shifts you do, the greater the risk.

Many people would say you can adapt to night shift work and lower the risks involved over time. In conversations with shiftworkers, many shiftworkers will self-report achieving even more sleep during the day than at night, with some workers reporting up to nine hours of quality sleep. Using an actigraphy device (wearable device) to collect longitudinal data, we (the authors) have yet to observe any evidence of these claims.

4.9   Can people adjust to just working the night shift?

Researchers explored whether permanent night shift workers biologically adapt to the night shift[87] based on their melatonin rhythm. They found that less than 3% of permanent night workers had an adjustment of their melatonin rhythm to night work, which would be evidence of biological adaptation to night shift work.

We are biologically not designed to work on a permanent night shift roster, and the vast majority of shiftworker will never fully adapt to the night shift[82]. In addition, within this group, we don't know the full extent of permanent night shift work on long-term health problems. The World Health Organisation has classified shiftwork as a type 2A carcinogen (highly probable). In particular, those working permanent night shifts have an increase in the odds risk ratio of developing cancer. The information in this book and our online courses are aimed at educating and informing people and shiftworkers to reduce this risk through improving sleep, managing sleep disorders and improving performance.

Permanent night shift also affects personal relationships and social and family life. When working whilst everyone is asleep and sleeping whilst everyone is awake, it can feel like you're living a life of opposites with friends, family, and loved ones. This may also lead to social isolation and difficulty engaging in sporting activities with others or participating in a team-based sport[38].

4.10 What is the best direction or rotation of a shift or roster system?

The rotation or direction of shifts is challenging for the shift worker and the roster designer. Factors to consider are preferences, lifestyle or family circumstances. Many shiftworkers or those working irregular hours don't want to spend their time off work recovering from night shifts. Rotating shifts refer to various work schedules and signify shifts that rotate or change according to a schedule. Shifts can rotate forward (morning, evening, night) or backward (night, evening, morning). Typically, these shifts are 8, 10 or 12 hrs in duration. The direction of scheduling is essential in designing a shift and roster system.

Circadian principles support forward rotating shifts: the human circadian timing system operates slightly longer than a 24 hr day[23]. Work schedules that move forward in time (days to nights) are, therefore, more accessible and less physiologically stressful for the body because they follow the body's natural tendency towards a day longer than 24 hrs. Compared to the favourable forward rotation, backward rotations (nights to days) are associated with self-reported increased recovery and overall poor health[88], more complaints of inadequate sleep, health problems and lack of social time[23,88]. In addition, backward-rotating rosters also have increased sickness, injury, higher blood pressure, fatigue and changes in glucose[89].

Scientific insight: direction of the roster design

A study was conducted, examining 4,750 shiftworkers working a rotating 3-shift system at three electronics manufacturing plants (day work from 6:00 to 14:00, evening work from 14:00 to 22:00, night work from 22:00 to 06:00). The shiftworkers reported that their sleep quality when working a forward operating roster was better, however, those <30 years of age coped better with the backward rotation compared to those >30 years of age. It is worth noting that this study is limited to self-reported sleep quality, and no objective measure of sleep was obtained using external devices or apparatus. However, the strength is an extremely high number of shiftworkers participating[90].

In a separate study of Italian nurses, 50 people worked a forward operating roster, and 50 people worked a backward operating roster. Those nurses working the forward operating roster slept longer by nearly 1:30 hrs per night, had less awakening during sleep, less disturbance during work and less interference with social and family life. In contrast, those working backward rotating shift schedules had less sleep, more sleep disturbances and less work-life balance[89].

4.11   What is the impact of consecutive work shifts on fatigue?

While long-duration work shifts can cause fatigue and impaired performance, an additional concern is that the long-duration work shift can be repeated many times, resulting in chronic sleep loss and a build-up of *"sleep debt"* (i.e., sleep insufficiency). This is known to cause a cumulative build-up of fatigue and associated performance deficits. For instance, laboratory studies have shown that two weeks of six hrs of sleep produces a performance deficit comparable to one whole night without sleep[6], which, as described above, is associated with the same impairment induced by double the legal limit of alcohol[28]. Moreover, as the build-up of fatigue is incremental, workers are less aware of their sleepiness[6].

In a combined assessment of several studies, Folkard examined the increase in relative risk of an accident for each successive night shift worked. Here, the relative risk increased ~6% on the second night (compared to the first), 17% on the third night, and 36% on the fourth night[37].

4.12 How do I manage the transition to night shifts, between and post-night shifts?

Many shiftworkers struggle with adaptation to the first night shift and report that it is the most difficult for them to adjust to and the most difficult for them to complete tasks and get through the night. If you are a night shift worker, transitioning successfully to your first night shift is essential. It is important to know that everyone is different, and you may need to adjust some of this guidance based on personal preference or circumstances. Consider the following points as you prepare for the night shift:

Sleep optimisation is beneficial before the night shift. Aim to get several good nights of sleep in the proceeding 24, 48 and 72 hrs before the night shift.

Where possible, **adjust your sleep-wake behaviours** before night shifts, maybe sleep in a little longer, even if it's just for an extra hour. This technique can be impossible for those working a rotating roster where you jump from days to nights and back again quickly as you may already be at work.

Have a lie-in on the morning before your first night shift. We aim to increase your sleep before the first night shift and reduce any existing sleep debt.

Napping before the night shift may be a good strategy. These can be long naps (i.e., 4 hrs). Be aware that if you nap for 30-40 mins, your body will enter deep sleep. The advantage of deep sleep is that it will help to reduce sleep debt, but it can take around an hour to be fully alert again, so allow time to wake up afterwards. Understanding the timing of such sleep is vital. The best times will be 13:00-16:00 if your shift starts between 17:00-19:00 and 21:00-23:00 if your shift starts at midnight.

Napping will be most challenging during the forbidden or wake maintenance zones (WMZ) from 17:00 to 20:00.

Sleep environment: Sleeping during the day can be challenging. Make your bedroom as dark, quiet, and comfortable as possible to promote quality sleep during the daytime. Consider using blackout curtains, white noise, and earplugs to minimise noise and consider an eye mask to eliminate all light. Air temperature and airflow may also be helpful; air conditioning or fans may benefit some people.

Diet and nutrition: Avoidance of alcohol in the 24 hrs before the night shift will be beneficial in maintaining good sleep quality. Caffeine should be used strategically and would be best to be consumed during the night shift before midnight to get the best effect on alertness and to minimise the impact on the day next sleep. Ensure you have eaten before the first night shift (main meal). Whilst eating during the night shift, pay attention to hydration levels, consume small snacks throughout the night and aim not to consume more than 600 calories. When you finish the night shift, have a protein-rich breakfast before sleep. Avoid large meals as it may impact sleep quality.

Physical activity is also a great way to prepare for the night shift; many people enjoy going outside, swimming, swimming, or cycling. Such activity may help boost your energy levels, improve mood, and promote better sleep quality. However, avoid vigorous exercise too close to a nap before the first night shift or at the end of a night shift. Light to moderate exercise may be fine for most people.

4.13 How to rest between each night shift

When you complete the night shift, aim to avoid **sunlight or artificial light** before going to bed as much as possible, and consider wearing sunglasses if it is safe to do so.

Eat a **light breakfast** when you have the same shift for at least a few days and eat a meal or snack at the same time each day to promote regular body cycles. If you work nights for several days, eat "lunch" mid-way through your shift.

A **biphasic approach to sleep** may be required. If you're a natural early bird, try 3-4 hrs to reduce your sleep debt. If you're a night owl, you'll find it more challenging to sleep in the afternoon but try at least a 15–20 mins nap before you get ready for work. If you nap for 30-40 mins, your body will enter deep sleep, and you may have sleep inertia or grogginess upon waking. In general, after a nightshift:

- Go to sleep as soon as you can

- Aim to get at least 6 hrs of sleep (between 7 am – 1 pm)

- Maintain a cool, dark, and quiet environment (Use earplugs and an eye mask while sleeping)

- Consider relaxation techniques, breathing, stretching, yoga, and meditation

- Avoid alcohol, caffeine, and heavy meals before sleeping

- No alcohol after the night shift

- Eat a small to medium meal, hydrate, and don't go to bed hungry or thirsty

- Eliminate all-natural light sources

4.14 How to maintain alertness on nightshift

- **Lighting:** Increase lighting levels in offices, workshops and dimly lit areas. The brighter, the better

- **Noise:** conversation with colleagues, background sound

- **Exercise/activity:** before/during night shift

- **Mental stimulation:** mentally stimulating tasks/activities & taking breaks when performing boring or repetitive tasks

- **Caffeine:** early during the night shift limit/avoid; if you have trouble falling/staying asleep, avoid caffeine within 4 hrs of planned bedtime. Caffeinated drinks like tea and coffee can be helpful stimulants to promote attention in the first half of a shift. However, taking within a few hours of bedtime could result in a longer time to fall asleep, reduced deep sleep and fewer sleep hours

- **Diet:** minimise large meals at night & stick to a healthy diet

- **Napping:** short naps before and during the night but be wary of sleep inertia & nap in a safe place. A mid-shift power nap of up to 30-40 mins is more effective than coffee for improving alertness

4.15 Recovering after the final nightshift

- Eat a light breakfast before sleeping

- Have a long nap (i.e. for 2-3 hrs) after last night's shift, not a full sleep. This may not always be possible, depending on if you have to travel home from a remote location, such as fly in, fly out or drive in drive out

- Be mindful that you are in sleep debt

- Get bright light exposure during the day after the last night shift. Natural light is the best way to synchronise back into a normal daytime routine

- Go outside and get exposure to sunlight

- Go to bed at a regular time (e.g., 22:00)

- Particularly important for evening chronotypes

4.16 General strategies to support you as a shiftworker

- Maintain a good fitness level (aerobic exercise 3-4 times per week for 30-40 mins and 2-3 strength or resistance exercise sessions per week)

- Keep weight in a healthy range (Body Mass Index 18-25)

- Strive for engaged coping strategies

- Positive attitude and social interactions

4.17 Does my commute duration to and from work affect my sleep when doing shiftwork?

Commuting is a broad term and can mean many things. In shiftwork, we refer to commuting as the daily travel to and from the workplace. Therefore, for most people, there will be two parts to the commute:

- On the way to the workplace

- On the way home

People often ask, *"what is the safest limit for a commute time?", Should my commute be <30 mins, <1 hr or is 90 mins okay as I must live 100km from my workplace due to house prices?"*

The way to approach this problem is risk-based. The first aspect we should look at is the shift length. The shift length is an essential aspect. When we subtract the shift length from 24 hrs, we are left with the available time for rest, sleep, family time, eating, exercise and the commute. In that context, let us look at three examples.

Example 1: 8 hr shift worker, they have a remaining 16 hrs. If we subtract 8 hrs for sleep, 2 hrs for family time, exercise, and to eat, they are left with an additional 6 hrs of time. Therefore, technically, they could commute each way up to 3 hrs.

Example 2: 10 hr shift worker, they have a remaining 14 hrs. If we subtract 8 hrs for sleep, 2 hrs for family time, exercise, and eating, they are left with an additional 4 hrs of time. Therefore, technically, they could commute each way up to 2 hrs.

Example 3: 12 hr shift worker they have a remaining 12 hrs. If we subtract 8 hrs for sleep, 2 hrs for family time, exercise, and to eat, they are left with an additional 2 hrs of time. Therefore, technically they could commute each way for up to 1 hr.

These three examples are mathematically based on the number of hours a day. Let us further explore the potential risks of commuting. The next factor to consider is the shift type.

Is the person undertaking a day, evening, or night shift?

The risk will generally be lower when undertaking the day shift as all the work activity is during daylight hours. However, the risk is significantly increased if the commute begins before 06:00. This is based on biological factors. So even with our 8 hr shift workers who may commute 3 hrs, if they must start a day shift at 07:00, they must leave home at 04:00, putting them in the middle of the most pronounced circadian nadir of a 24 hr period when reaction time, both temperature and sleep inertia is at its highest. This may also result in sleep loss. To achieve the recommended 8 hrs of sleep per night based upon a 04:00 commute departure, they must awaken at 3:30 to get ready. Therefore, requiring a bedtime of 19:00 the previous day to allow for sleep onset. This poses another problem as the person must fall asleep during the wake maintenance or forbidden zones. This is the most challenging time to fall asleep within 24 hrs. So, in this case, the best advice would be for the shift worker to limit their commute to 1 hr, require a time of wake at 05:30 to depart at 06:00.

Why does shiftwork become more challenging as I get older?

"I can't hack it like I used to"

We hear many reports and stories from older shift workers (>35 years of age) about some wild roster schedules they worked in the past. When asked how they managed, the answer often is something like *"I was young… I wouldn't be able to do it now"*. Indeed, there is truth to this statement. Many scientific studies have shown that younger adults are generally better able to cope with the demands of shiftwork and adjust better to rotating shift patterns and night shifts than their older counterparts. But why is this the case?

We don't completely know why shiftwork becomes more difficult as we age. We do, however, know that it's likely due to a cocktail of factors rather than just one. Below, we talk about two of these factors; however, many more likely play a part (e.g., increased cortisol levels with age).

Natural changes to our body clock

The properties of our circadian rhythm, or our internal body clock, do not stay the same as we progress from infancy to adulthood. For the first two months of a baby's life, they do not have a fully developed circadian rhythm[91], leading them to sleep all day. Additionally, biological and environmental factors cause an increase in evening tendencies for adolescents and young adults[92]. This tendency makes nightshift work easier to adapt to, as there is already a drive to delay bed and wake times. However, we see the opposite with older adults: a natural drive toward morningness[93], making it far more challenging to deal with the demands of night shift work.

Along with a shift to earlier schedules, we see a decrease in older individuals' ability to phase shift or adapt their circadian rhythm such that they can wake up, be alert, and go to sleep at times that are appropriate for any given shift[94]. Changes to our eyes and vision as we age may play a part as visual degradation and impairments can worsen the ability to cope with shiftwork[95,96].

As we age, we see an overall weaker circadian drive or influence of the body clock on sleep behaviour. Without a strong biological signal informing us when to be asleep and when to be awake, it may cause an older individual to have shorter periods of sleep and use daytime napping more (napping becomes more frequent as we age[97]) to accomplish our overall required amount of sleep. As long (often 12+ hrs) workdays don't usually allow for much napping opportunity, this natural method of catching up on our daily sleep needs becomes lost, making older shift workers feel more tired and at a higher fatigue risk.

Increased rates of sleep disorders/disturbances for shiftworkers

Poorer sleep means more daytime fatigue and weariness. Hence, when fatigue due to disordered or disturbed sleep is added on top of fatigue experienced due to shift change and night shift work, accompanied by sleep disturbances, it can be unbearable for some individuals, placing them under extreme fatigue risk.

Rates of disturbed and disordered sleep generally increase with age. One study found the odds of having insomnia to increase by 1.1 for every decade of life [98], while the rates of Obstructive Sleep Apnea increase each year until the age of 65. At that point, it is 2-3 times more prevalent than for middle-aged adults [99]. Another age-related sleep disturbance is nocturia (waking up regularly in the night to pee), which is potentially the number one source of poor sleep in older adults [100]. Hence, shiftwork can become more difficult for older individuals, as they are more likely to experience disturbed or disordered sleep, which can compound the sleep disturbances associated with shiftwork.

Regular aerobic exercise may help protect from age-related circadian changes. A study in 2016 compared healthy older individuals (~60 years old on average) with different aerobic capabilities (VO_2 max) and found that those with greater aerobic capacity also had stronger circadian rhythms, were less active at night, more vigilant throughout the day [101].

4.18 Practical tips for shiftworkers

- Coping with shiftwork becomes more difficult with age. Investing time and effort in preparing for shift changes/ night shifts becomes increasingly important before undertaking them. You may think of this in the same way as having to spend a little longer warming up before exercise to avoid injury as you get older

- If you have found yourself increasingly struggling to cope with shiftwork as you age, exploring permanent day shift options with your leader/ manager is worthwhile

- With regards to the increase in sleep disorder prevalence with age, addressing lifestyle factors (i.e., diet, exercise, alcohol) and seeking treatment for physical and mental health conditions may improve one's ability to cope with shiftwork

4.19 How does being on call impact my sleep?

On-call work refers to working conditions whereby workers can be called to work during the designated work period (day or night). This is common for medical staff, utility workers, fire and rescue, military and many more. In between calls, workers can be free to go about their daily lives, including sleep. The evidence suggests that workers have a poorer sleep period when on-call[102], regardless of whether they receive a call[103-106]. Shorter sleep times while on-call have been reported across business sectors, including railway engineers[106] and electricity and gas supply workers[107].

Scientific insight: the impact of on call work on next-day performance

Laboratory simulation of an on-call night shift shows that workers take longer to fall asleep, have increased night-time awakenings and have lighter sleep[108]; this may be worse when the likelihood of the call is uncertain[109]. Given the impact of an on-call shift on sleep, this can lead to fatigue the next day and reduce fitness for work.

4.20 Practical application for managing on-call

- As such, on-call shifts should be taken into consideration when planning rosters

- A minimum break of 8 hrs should be considered on completion of a call out overnight before returning to work the next day

4.21 The importance of prioritising sleep for leaders

When we think about sleep and the workplace, most people's mind immediately goes to worker safety and fatigue. This is because there is a of research related to this topic as we have been discussing. However, our thinking should not be limited to the people working on the ground regarding sleep loss. Leaders get tired, and it is well established that fatigue resulting from sleep loss can negatively influence decision-making. As an extreme example, managers had "minimal sleep" the night before they decided to override warnings and unsafely launch the U.S. Space Shuttle Challenger in 1986, resulting in the death of all seven crew members [110]. Beyond poor decision-making, however, how does sleep interact with a leader's ability to lead?

Scientific insight: how do leaders tend to sleep, and what are their general attitudes/ beliefs about sleep?

An interesting study [111] explored this topic by surveying almost 400 senior professionals and leaders across 38 countries. Across this population, the average self-reported sleep duration was 6 hrs and 36 mins, while the modal (most common) sleep duration for high-performing executives was only six hours! These leaders recognised that this was almost an hour less than what they needed. However, it must be stressed that self-reported sleep duration is almost always overestimated (usually by 20 – 30 mins) so these amounts are well of those considered healthy for most adults.

Perhaps more concerning than these numbers, however, are some of the attitudes shared by these executives and business leaders about sleep; a quarter of responders agreed that sacrificing sleep is necessary to get ahead in their work, and about a third of leaders agreed that high performers do not need much sleep. These sentiments are scary but should not be overly surprising, given the all-too-common sayings *"sleep is for the weak,"* and *"money never sleeps."*

4.22 Leaders are not sleeping enough; how does this impact their ability to lead?

While there is not a lot of literature on this compared to, say, worker safety, the work that is out there does not paint a pretty picture of this scenario. Some studies exploring sleep loss and leadership have often done so within the lens of the Ego Depletion Model; this model essentially suggests that self-control is a finite resource that is depleted when we use it, and when we sleep less, we tend to run on empty for this resource a lot more. It is through this ego depletion that reduced sleep quality (but interestingly, not sleep quantity) tends to lead to more abusive supervisory behaviour, according to data from Barnes and colleagues [112].

Importantly for businesses and other organisations, this 'abusive behaviour' leads to less work engagement. In a separate study, individuals who slept less experienced greater ego depletion, which actually led them to more unethical behaviours, measured both subjectively (rated by supervisors) and objectively (higher likelihood of lying about test results in order to gain a prize) [113].

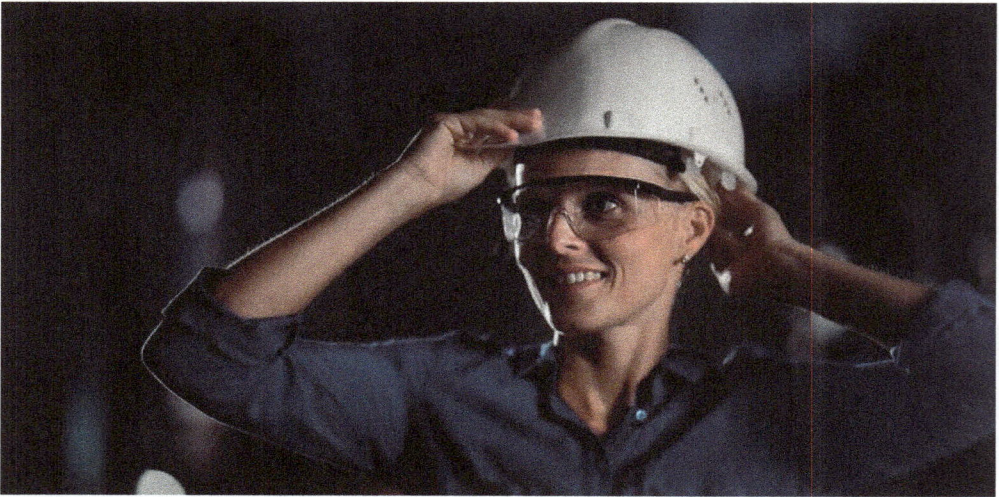

Sleep loss also degrades leadership abilities through emotional changes. A 2016 study found that individuals who slept for just under 5 hours gave less charismatic speeches [114]. Furthermore, a 2017 study on 109 business leaders found that poorer sleep quality and quantity were associated with poorer emotional and social competence [115], and the less a leader slept, the more hostile their followers found them, leading to a poorer overall relationship quality [116].

Tired leaders tend to be boring, grumpy, and potentially abusive, with poor emotional intelligence and substandard relationships with those they lead. They also have a higher chance of making ethically questionable decisions. This is in addition to the known negative effects of sleep loss on decision-making, which is of obvious importance for leaders making big decisions.

4.23 How can leaders change this?

How can we avoid adopting these obviously bad characteristics? Well, the first step would be to disown the cancerous sleep is for the weak mindset that is pervasive among leaders in all occupations. One respondent in Nowack's research stated that

> *"In a macho leadership culture, admitting you need sleep is weakness."*

To me, all the abovementioned negative effects of poor sleep are characteristics of a weak leader. Very specifically on the topic of weak leadership, a study investigating [117] acute sleep restriction (5 nights of 2-2.5 hrs sleep) led naval officers to adopt "passive-avoidant" leadership styles, avoiding challenges/difficulty and just waiting for mistakes to happen instead of proactive and inspiring leadership approaches. The results of this quite strongly suggest that while sleep does not make you a weak leader, dismissing sleep does.

Ensuring your sleep hygiene is in shape would be the first point of call; this includes ensuring that your bedroom is cool and dark, you are avoiding stimulating activities such as reading and responding to emails at least half an hour before bed, and you are avoiding caffeine 6-8 hours out from bedtime. If issues persist, it would be recommended to see a sleep physician, as an underlying sleep disorder may be preventing progress.

Want to know more about sleep and leadership?

Season 9 Episode 1: Sleep and Leadership with Professor Chris Barnes. In the episode on sleep and leadership, Ian speaks with Professor Chris Barnes. Chris is an international expert on the relationship between sleep, fatigue, and leadership in business.

LISTEN HERE:
https://sleep4performance.com/podcast/s9-ep01-sleep-and-leadership/

OR SCAN QR CODE

Commuting, Travel Fatigue, and Jet Lag

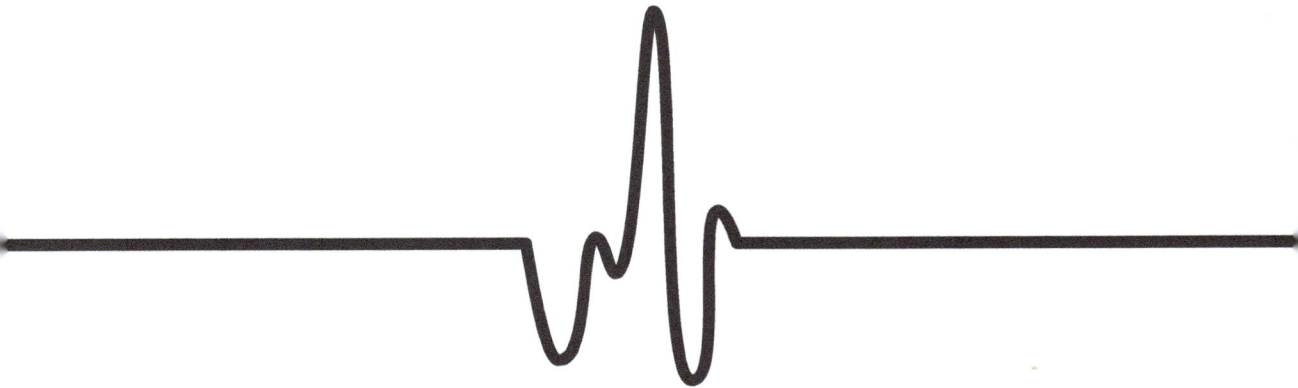

5. Commuting, Travel Fatigue, and Jet Lag

5.1 Commuting

Commuting to work, a seemingly routine activity, can pose significant risks. In Australia, 20-30% of all vehicle incidents are estimated to be due to fatigue[118]. This risk is increased during certain times of the day; driving in the early morning is associated with increased accident risk, affecting professional drivers and those who commute to work[119]. Additionally, driving home from night shifts is associated with increased commute risk.

It is useful to place commuting into two categories:

- Commuting via trains, buses or public transport means that individual fatigue does not impact commute safety. However, individual fatigue and sleepiness may remain high as the person has to wake early and usually cannot sleep (or at least obtain quality sleep) during the commute. We use the term **"passive"** commute for this type of commute

- Commuting via driving means that individual fatigue directly impacts commute safety. Thus, the risk of motor vehicle incidents is increased when fatigued. We use the term **"active"** commute for this type of commute

5.2 Practical application for driving

When driving during a work shift, it is essential to factor in breaks.

- Meal breaks within 5 hrs of the shift

- Short fatigue breaks at least every 2 hrs. It may be useful to think of these fatigue breaks in a gold, silver, and bronze manner:

  - Gold: Napping for 20-30 minutes within the break

- ◆ Silver: Getting some fresh air and getting blood flowing with some movement or light physical activity outside of the vehicle

- ◆ Bronze: Doing anything other than driving for 15 mins or more

- More frequent breaks may be helpful on the night shift

- If two people are driving, share the driving load

- Caffeine can be a useful fatigue countermeasure (or tool to reduce fatigue risk) while driving. However, we note that:

  - ◆ If sleep is to be attempted within 6 hrs of the commute, it may be wise to consider all other strategies before caffeine, as caffeine can interfere with sleep

  - ◆ Some people are relatively unaffected by caffeine: if you are someone who can fall asleep easily following a cup of coffee, then caffeine is unlikely to be a useful strategy for keeping you awake and alert while driving

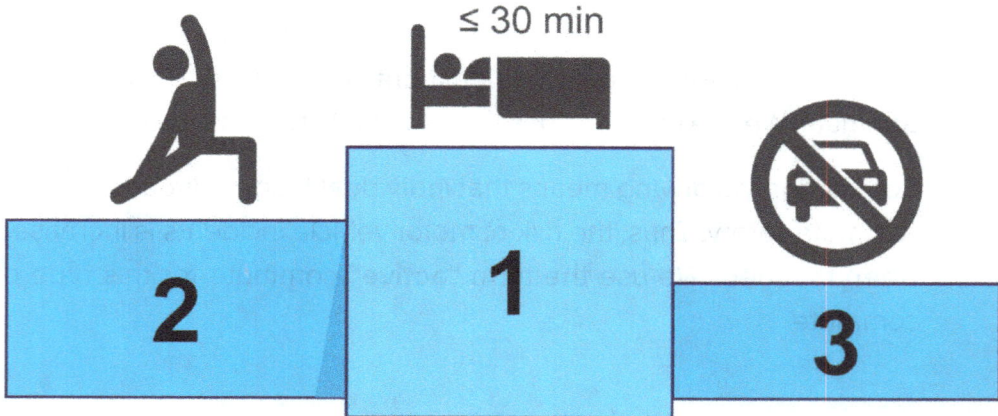

Figure 18. The Gold, Silver, and Bronze Options for Fatigue Breaks while Driving

5.3 Questions to ask yourself before or during your commute

- How much have I slept over the last 24, 48 and 72 hrs? Have I had at least 6, 12, 18 hrs of sleep over this time?

- What type of activity am I doing? Am I driving short or long distances (for example, commercial driving)?

- Have I been awake for the last >17 hrs? If so, this is a high risk, and your cognitive performance and reaction time may be similar to someone with a blood alcohol concentration of 0.05%

- What is the time? Research suggests that driving during the window of circadian low (WOCL: 03:00 to 06:00 for most people) is linked to an increase in incident risk

- What is the environment I am driving in like? Am I on a dull, monotonous drive with long and straight roads? If so, the commute risk from fatigue is amplified[120]

- Is there an alternative to driving if I am tired? Can I stop or take a nap or rest break? Can someone pick me up? If I am tired, the safest decision I can make is not to drive

5.4 Risk factors for fatigue-related crashes

The existing scientific literature (both Australian and international) highlights several groups that are at higher risk of fatigue-related crashes[118].

These groups include:

- Younger drivers

- Male drivers

- Shift workers

- Drivers with sleep disorders or medical conditions

- Professional drivers (for example, truck drivers, delivery drivers, or taxi drivers)

- New parents

Whilst fatigue-related crashes are not restricted to these groups alone, the higher prevalence of fatigue-related crashes in these groups suggests that they should be especially cognisant of their fatigue and take extra precautions to reduce fatigue-related commute risk.

5.5   Microsleeps

Microsleeps are brief, involuntary lapses into sleep. They typically last between 3-15 seconds [121]. However, even microsleeps shorter than three seconds can have catastrophic outcomes. Microsleeps can occur while driving, undertaking a safety-critical task, or during an activity that requires your attention. You may appear awake during a microsleep, and your co-workers or friends may not notice it. Much of the time, you will not recall or remember having a microsleep after the event. They are more prevalent during the WOCL and when a person is sleep-deprived [122]. However, they can occur anywhere and at any time. Unlike some other events that may briefly take your attention off the road or away from a task (changing the air conditioner temperature or responding to someone over the radio, for example), you can't choose when you have a microsleep; it could occur when stopped at a red light or approaching a red light at high speed.

5.6   Travel fatigue and jet lag

Managing travel and jet lag is extremely important. Many people report that when they undertake long bouts of travel across three or more time zones (interstate/province or internationally), they feel sleepy, sluggish, tired and unable to perform at their best. These feelings and changes are due to travel-related body-clock disruptions and go away only when the individual has adapted to the new time zone.

The problems can be further worsened by temperature extremes and high altitudes at the destination, underlying sleep disorders (which are predicted to affect 22% of the Australian population), advancing age, excessive body weight, training or workload, stress, digestive issues, or respiratory problems. Managing these factors is very important for minimising any negative effects experienced with large bouts of travel.

When discussing travel, fatigue, and jet lag, it is essential to distinguish between *"travel fatigue"* and *"jet lag"*. We will use the term *"travel"* to describe a journey to a destination. This can be through any mode of transport, such as a car, bus, train, ferry, or air travel.

5.7 What is "travel fatigue"?

Travel fatigue can be attributed to the following factors: frequency of travel, duration of travel, cumulative travel and timing of travel. Travel fatigue results in generalised fatigue, occasional headaches, mental weariness, and often a distorted sleep routine. It can also lead to illness, changes in mood and motivation, and decreases in performance [123,124].

Travel fatigue may occur due to:

- Stress and logistics associated with travel

- Being in a confined space with limited movement for an extended period of time

- Noise and disruption due to the travel modality or other passengers

- The inability to sleep (or obtain quality sleep) due to the previous two points

- Exposure to dry air, possibly causing dehydration [125]

An important distinction is that travel fatigue does not depend on the number of time zones crossed. It can occur after northbound or southbound travel. Getting good sleep generally reduces the symptoms of travel fatigue [126]. However, with many travel bouts in a short period of time, the negative effects of travel fatigue can build and result in poor health and well-being.

5.8 What is jet lag?

Jet lag is a circadian rhythm disorder that is a temporary condition that is alleviated over time, from one day to up to two weeks for some individuals [127]. The current diagnostic criteria for jet lag include:

- Excessive daytime sleepiness or insomnia-like symptoms associated with rapid travel over at least two time zones

- Worsened daytime functioning, apathy or somatic symptoms (for example, gastrointestinal disturbance), at least within 1-2 days after travel

- These symptoms or disturbances cannot be attributed to anything else

Crossing multiple time zones in either an easterly (e.g., Los Angeles to New York, United States of America) or westerly direction (London, England to New York, US) causes jet lag. Travelling from south to north within the same or similar time zone (Perth, Australia to Beijing, China) may cause fatigue to an individual due to the time spent travelling or acute sleep disruption from an overnight flight. **However, these effects are due to travel fatigue and not jet lag.**

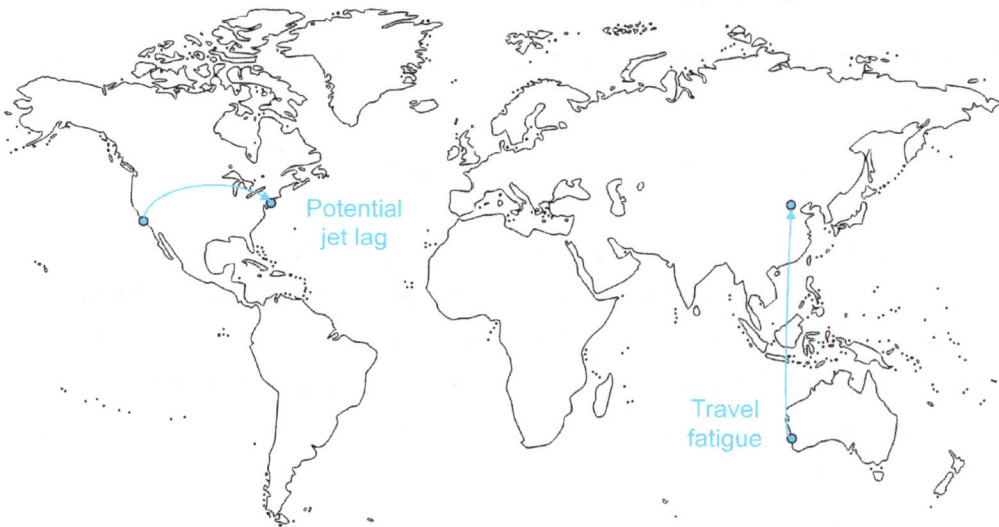

Figure 19. Travel Fatigue vs Jet Lag

Figure note: different air travel commutes. One crosses three time zones, and thus has the potential to lead to jet lag. The other crosses no time zones and, therefore, cannot lead to jet lag; any negative symptoms following the travel period must be due to travel fatigue.

Whenever >3 time zones are crossed, disagreements between the body's internal clock and the clock on the wall can wreak havoc if not properly managed. To get a grip on this issue, consider that humans have several internal physiological processes that affect sleepiness and performance. These are typically tuned to a well-synchronised 24 hr rhythm, kept right on schedule by the timing of sunlight exposure (at least if wake times, daytime activity, and nightly bedtimes are somewhat consistent).

In this situation, the body's time and the environmental time are closely aligned, and the body's rhythms are in harmony. But when travel-related time changes occur, problems arise because the body's sense of time does not match time cues in the new environment, mainly light; however, meal timing, exercise timing and social cues also seem important. Since this is a phenomenon of modern airline transportation, it has been labelled *"jet lag"*.

A general rule of thumb is that you should allow 1 day to adjust for every time zone crossed when travelling eastward. A trip from London, United Kingdom, to Perth, Australia, which is in an easterly direction, may take up to 8 days. Travelling westward is normally slightly easier, and the rule of thumb in this scenario is that you should allow ½ day for every time zone crossed to adjust. A trip from London, United Kingdom, to New York may only take 2 ½ to 3 days as there are 5 time zones crossed.

5.9 Myths about jet lag

Some think and say that you need two hours of sleep for every hour you fly to get rid of jet lag. No scientific evidence supports this, particularly when you are travelling within the same time zone during regular daylight hours. On some popular podcasts, it is often said that exercise is the best way to eliminate jet lag on arrival. However, if you arrive at a destination at 3 am (during the WOCL), then it may be best to sleep and exercise later in the morning outdoors with access to sunlight.

5.10   What strategies can I use to help with jet lag and/or travel fatigue?

Melatonin

Exogenous (external from the body) melatonin is both a chronobiotic and a hypnotic, meaning it can shift the timing of the circadian system [128]. However, it can also make falling and staying asleep easier [129]. The time of day that exogenous melatonin is taken significantly impacts its effects. For example, if ingested at night when endogenous melatonin is high, exogenous melatonin will not increase sleepiness [130]. Conversely, exogenous melatonin will increase drowsiness if consumed during the day (when endogenous melatonin is low) [131]. Exogenous melatonin use has been shown to effectively shift the circadian clock and reduce jet lag [130], however, should be used with care; if taken at the wrong time, it can do as much harm as it can do good for your sleep and jet lag.

Action: Specifically, if you are required to phase advance (shift your body clock earlier), melatonin should be taken in the afternoon; if you are required to phase delay (move your body clock later), melatonin should be taken in the morning, before attempting to sleep (or return to sleep).

Caffeine

Caffeine is readily available in many forms, including tablets, gums, candies, beverages and foods. An 8-fl oz cup of drip-brewed coffee contains an average of 135 mg of caffeine, an 8-fl oz cup of brewed tea contains approximately 50 mg of caffeine, and a 12-fl oz cola drink has an average of 44 mg of caffeine. However, these are just averages, and caffeine content can vary greatly depending on the source; for example, 8-fl oz cups of Starbucks coffee have been measured to contain 250 mg of caffeine! Endogenous (or natural) melatonin secretion is delayed consistently by 40 min when 200 mg of caffeine is taken 3 hr before bedtime[132]. Caffeine has been reported to help adjust to new time zones (and thus reduce jet lag), when consumed at an appropriate time for the new time zone[133]. However again, be careful to not consume caffeine too close to your desired bed time, as it can delay sleep and reduce sleep quality. Recent research shows that caffeine from coffee may impact your sleep when consumed within 8.8 hrs of bedtime[134], and more caffeine-rich sources (like a pre-workout supplement) can impact your sleep even if you had more than 13 hrs before bedtime.

Action: When travelling, stop consuming coffee within 8 to 9 hrs of your desired bedtime to ensure you can fall asleep. Caffeine may be used as an aid to stay awake prior to this point and may help accelerate the time it takes to re-synchronise your body clock to the destination time (if taken in the morning of the destination time zone, for example).

Water

While drinking water cannot reduce jet lag, it can reduce travel fatigue, which is often mistaken for jet lag as it commonly occurs after a long flight. Furthermore, some of the symptoms of jet lag, such as headaches and gut issues, may worsen if you are dehydrated. Therefore, it is essential to stay hydrated while flying since dehydration can be exacerbated due to pressure and dry cabin air[134].

Action: Slightly higher than regular fluid intake is recommended due to the above-mentioned environmental conditions, as is avoiding alcohol while flying[135-137]. Frequent sips of non-alcoholic and non-carbonated drinks: water (best), fruit juice, or carbohydrate-containing drinks based on individual energy/caloric.

Alcohol

One of the most common strategies people use to help them sleep on flights is a bit of alcohol. But does alcohol actually help us relax and fall asleep? Along with caffeine, it is one of the most widely consumed psychoactive drugs today. Alcohol has been shown, even at low doses (1-2 drinks), to reduce the time it takes to fall asleep, which may explain why people take it to fall asleep. This may be viewed as a positive. However, alcohol has several negative impacts once a person has fallen asleep:

- An increase in **awakenings** during the night

- **Less stage 3, Non-Rapid Eye Movement**, or N3 sleep. We know that this stage of sleep is extremely important for brain functioning and physical recovery

- Early in a sleep period, it takes **longer for us to get into Rapid Eye Movement** (REM) sleep. If the amount of alcohol consumed is not too large, a *"REM rebound"* can occur in the second half of the sleep, often resulting in many vivid dreams

- If the amount of alcohol consumed is very large, there is an overall reduction in REM sleep throughout the night, which is important for brain functioning

- An **increase in snoring** and other sleep-related breathing disorders[138]

- It can lead to increased **fatigue and dehydration**

Action: We recommend avoiding alcohol both during flights and immediately after flying to avoid worsening travel fatigue and jet lag symptoms.

5.11 Sleeping pills

Trying to sleep while travelling can be difficult. Often, opportunities to sleep may arise at times when it is naturally difficult to fall asleep (i.e., between 08:00 and 12:00 or between 16:00 and 20:00 in the departure location time zone). Even when not at these times, the sleep environment is often uncomfortable (i.e., hot, cold, noisy, or brightly lit, coupled with an inability to lay down horizontally), and stress/ anxiety can be raised. These environmental conditions are unlikely sufficient to achieve quantity or quality sleep.

For these reasons, sleep-promoting hypnotics or sleep medications can be considered for situations with opportunities to sleep. Studies have shown that prescription hypnotics such as temazepam, zolpidem, eszopiclone, and zaleplon can be effective for falling asleep and staying asleep, even under less-than-optimal circumstances[139-141].

However, these medications should be used with caution as they can have lingering effects (e.g., drowsiness) and have been shown to interfere with natural sleep architecture[142]. Additionally, they will not stop the occurrence of jet lag, and sleepiness due to jet lag will still occur if there hasn't been a circadian adjustment to the new time zone. Lastly, we strongly advise against consistent use of these medications outside of specific circumstances, as issues around dependency and withdrawals can arise.

Action: If the aim is to sleep while travelling (which is appropriate if it is night-time at your destination), then sleeping pills may facilitate sleep when conditions do not allow for rest to occur naturally. Suppose you have trouble sleeping whilst travelling or initiating sleep at your destination. In that case, prescription hypnotics such as temazepam, zolpidem, eszopiclone, and zaleplon may be an appropriate tool for you.

5.12 Fibre-rich foods

Jet lag can lead to gastrointestinal disturbances for some people, which can be further worsened by dehydration, lack of movement, and nutrition changes, which are common during travel. Fibre-rich foods with natural laxative properties (e.g., prunes, kiwifruit, or chia seeds) have been recommended by some scientists to consume while travelling[135,136]. Consuming these foods won't reduce jet lag but may alleviate gastrointestinal disturbances, an often inconvenient symptom of jet lag. Additionally, foods high in carbohydrates can promote drowsiness and, if timed appropriately, may assist with promoting sleep. However, caution should be taken if you have any pre-existing issues regarding irritable bowel syndrome, Crohn's or other problems.

Action: Consuming fibre-rich foods with natural laxative properties (e.g., prunes, kiwifruit, or chia seeds) during travel (particularly air travel) may reduce gut discomfort.

Managing
Sleep

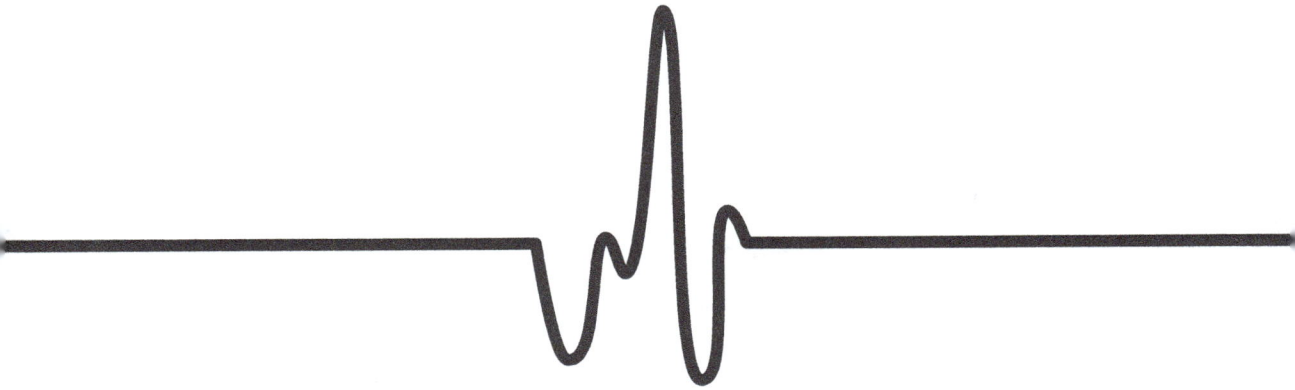

6. Managing Sleep

6.1 Why do I sleep better after a few (alcoholic) drinks?

One of the most common strategies that shiftworkers and people with insomnia or sleep problems use to help themselves fall asleep is alcohol. Shiftworkers, stressed-out athletes, leaders, parents, students, and many more swear by the positive effect of sinking a beer, sipping a glass of wine, or having a few shots of whisky to take the edge off after a hard day to help them unwind. But does alcohol help us to relax and fall asleep?

As discussed in the previous section, alcohol can decrease the time it takes to fall asleep, which might explain why some people drink it to *"help"* them sleep. However, alcohol consumption before bedtime can reduce overall sleep *quality* in many ways. These include:

- An increase in **awakenings** during the night

- **Less stage 3, Non-Rapid Eye Movement**, or N3 sleep. We know that this stage of sleep is extremely important for brain functioning and physical recovery

- Taking **longer to get into Rapid Eye Movement** (REM) sleep. If the amount of alcohol consumed is not too large, a *"REM rebound"* can occur in the second half of the sleep, often resulting in many vivid dreams. If the amount of alcohol consumed is considerable, there is an overall reduction in REM sleep throughout the night, which is essential for brain functioning

- An **increase in snoring** and other sleep-related breathing disorders[138]

- Increased **fatigue and dehydration**

Additionally, long-term use of alcohol by shiftworkers and those who struggle to fall asleep can lead to insomnia.

Scientific insights: alcohol use in shiftworkers

A study was conducted in 2022, exploring sleep and associated behavioural factors for shiftworkers within a remote mining operation in Western Australia. Using validated tools developed by the World Health Organisation, the researchers found that 36% of workers consumed alcohol at hazardous and harmful levels or were at risk of alcohol dependence [78].

In other research with nurses in Australia, Jillian Dorrian and Natalie Skinner report that 44% of nurses utilise alcohol as a sleep aid when working rotating shifts, with night shift workers more prone to increased levels of alcohol consumption [143].

Overall, the scientific research on shiftworkers and alcohol consumption indicates that shiftworkers, particularly those on night shift and rotating shifts, have more binge drinking behaviour, and those >50 years old are more at risk [144].

6.2 Practical application for alcohol consumption before sleep

If you have trouble falling asleep, some tips include:

- The use of relaxation techniques or guided meditation instead of alcohol consumption
- Substitute your alcoholic drink for a non-alcoholic drink; there are many non-alcoholic beers and beverages to choose from now.
- Increasing the time between your last drink and when you go to sleep
- Hydrating with water after consuming alcohol to reduce the negative impacts on your sleep

6.3 Is there a relationship between sleep and pain?

Many people who are in pain due to injury, illness, impairment or other reasons have problems with their sleep. It is currently estimated that >68% of people with chronic pain will have ongoing sleep problems [145].

But what causes what? Does the pain cause sleep issues, or do sleep issues lead to more pain?

Whilst long-term studies are needed, we currently understand that chronic pain is associated with sleep disturbances in a bidirectional manner (pain can lead to sleep issues, and sleep issues can lead to pain).

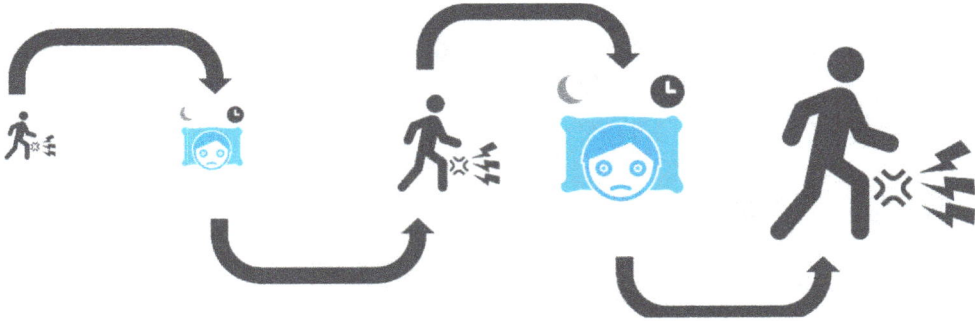

Figure 20. *Bidirectional Relationship with Sleep and Pain*

Figure note: The bidirectional relationship between sleep and pain. Pain can make sleep worse, which can make pain more severe, which can make sleep even worse, which can make pain even more severe!

Scientific insight: sleep and pain

A study randomly allocated participants to a 4 hr or 8 hr sleep opportunity for 12 days. Those who slept for 4 hrs a night had more body, back and stomach pain, were less optimistic and had poorer emotional well-being [146].

Another study found that when REM sleep (the stage of sleep where most of our dreams occur) was lost, people felt more pain. In another study, when people had their time in REM sleep reduced, they felt more pain the next day [147].

6.4   How does stress impact my sleep?

Stress can be defined as a state of worry or mental tension. We all experience stress in our lives. At the same time, stress isn't always negative; it is sometimes needed in appropriate doses to get things done. However, long-term exposure to stress may impact our sleep and overall health. Stress and the increasing cortisol levels (stress hormone) that come with it can affect our physical health, particularly while on night shift[148].

Scientific insight: stress and sleep in shiftworkers

In a study with 251 police officers who were shiftworkers completed a series of validated instruments assessing stress, health, and sleep. The research team found that shiftworkers had increased social stress, higher work discontent and sleep complaints, which led to poor sleep quality[149]. Similarly, in a study with 450 emergency nurses, 81% of participants had moderate stress, with this stress impacting their sleep quality[150].

Many organisations where shiftwork is conducted provide employee assistance programs to help workers manage psychological stressors. In addition, many community-based support mechanisms are in place.

6.5   Practical applications for stress reduction and sleep

- Identifying stressors in your life can be beneficial. Identify the most significant stressors and take action to address them

- Good sleep habits, such as having consistent bed and wake-up times, will also help

- Consider eliminating stimulants and alcohol during periods of stress to support focus during this time

- Exercise and natural light exposure are also recommended, as having these during the day can help sleep at night

- Mindfulness/ relaxation/ meditation/ breathing exercises can be helpful for some

- Have a *"mental holiday"* place

- Schedule *"worry time"* during the day

- Make a list of things to remember

- Avoid stressors within 1-2 hrs of bedtime

6.6   How does caffeine affect my sleep?

Being discovered nearly 3,000 years ago, caffeine is one of the oldest and most used psychoactive drugs out there! Caffeine is found naturally in a variety of foods and beverages. Caffeine (in the form of tea and coffee) is often consumed recreationally or as a quick pick-me-up in the afternoon. It is also commonly used as an anti-sleepiness tool, fatigue countermeasure, and as an aid for cognitive and physical performance. Caffeine has been shown to:

- Stimulate an increase in alertness and a reduction in fatigue

- Improve power and strength

- Increase metabolism and use fat better as a fuel source

This benefits humans in several ways:

- Improve reaction time and performance in some cognitively demanding tasks

- Improve performance in sports that require power and strength (like weightlifting or team sports like soccer and rugby) and endurance activities (like running and adventure racing)

Timing and dosage of caffeine are critical considerations. Caffeine consumption can affect sleep and lead to sleep loss, especially when consumed within 4 hrs of sleep. This is due to how caffeine interacts with the human body (this is called *pharmacokinetics*). The effect of caffeine peaks about 1 hr after consumption. However, the half-life of caffeine (the time it takes to get rid of half the caffeine from your system) can vary anywhere from 2-10 hrs between people, and it is commonly around 4-6 hrs. Therefore, caffeine's wake-promoting effects can last long after consumption. These effects include:

- Taking longer to fall asleep

- Waking up more throughout a night of sleep

- Spending more of an overall nighttime period awake

All of these effects can reduce the amount of sleep, and sleep loss can impair next-day performance. It is also worth noting that caffeine comes in many different forms. We tend to think about caffeine as just in coffee. However, caffeine is also in energy drinks, pre-workout powders, tea, sodas, and chocolate, the darker the chocolate, the higher the caffeine content.

Sources of Caffeine

Scientific insight: when to stop drinking caffeine

In 2023, Carrisa Gardiner conducted an extensive literature review and statistical analysis on all the current science of caffeine and sleep dating back as far as 1974 [151]. They found that caffeine consumed before bedtime results in taking longer to fall asleep, spending more time awake across the night, sleeping 45 mins less, and losing out on deep sleep. Some recommendations from this rigorous review are as follows:

1. To avoid effects on sleep, avoid coffee within approximately 8 hrs and 45 mins of your desired bedtime

2. Avoid pre-workout supplements (which usually contain very high amounts of caffeine) within 13 hrs and 15 mins of your desired bedtime

Want to know more about caffeine?

S4P Seminar 23: Check out Carissa Gardiner's presentation on the effect of caffeine on subsequent sleep. "Caffeine consumption in response to insufficient sleep may impair the onset and maintenance of subsequent sleep. This systematic review and meta-analysis investigated the effect of caffeine on the characteristics of nighttime sleep, intending to identify the time after which caffeine should not be consumed before bedtime."

LISTEN HERE:

https://youtu.be/wj1DBq12QWQ

OR SCAN QR CODE

6.7 Practical application for timing and managing caffeine consumption

- Try to limit coffee within 8 hrs and 45 mins of your desired bedtime, and avoid all caffeine within 4-6 hrs of your desired bedtime

- If you are working a night shift, stop all caffeine consumption after 03:00 at the latest. Caffeine consumed after this time will not help you stay awake; however, it can affect your sleep in the morning

- Caffeine affects people very differently. Be honest with yourself as to how it affects you and your sleep

6.8   What is the best nutrition strategy for shiftworkers?

What we eat is essential for our health, but when we eat is also very important. Circadian rhythms are often thought only to regulate when we are awake or asleep; however, they also influence other behaviours, including eating. For example, circadian rhythms increase our hunger in the evening and promote greater energy expenditure after a morning meal[152]. Like sleep, we have windows of time that are better or more appropriate for eating. Studies have shown that when both children and adults delay their bedtimes, they tend to eat more fast food and fattier foods, leading to higher overall caloric intake[153,154]. In addition, increased caloric intake later in the evening (after 8:00 pm) can increase body mass and body fat percentage[153,155]. Therefore, considering sleep and meal timings is worthwhile for effective weight loss or management; limiting food intake late in the evening is an excellent first step.

Shift work can result in a mismatch between natural eating windows (according to an individual's body clock) and actual eating windows. This mismatch or *"desynchronisation"* has been shown to increase ghrelin (a hormone that stimulates hunger) and decrease leptin levels (a hormone that signals that you are full), increasing appetite[152]. This is a potential contributing factor towards the increased risk of obesity, type 2 diabetes, heart disease and metabolic syndrome seen in shiftworkers[156].

Lifestyle factors, such as work and social events, often lead to large differences in both meal timing and sleep timing between weekdays and weekends. When looking at sleep and wake timing, this difference is called *"social jet lag"*. Social jet lag is considered a risk factor for metabolic health and obesity[157]. When looking at meal timing, the difference is called *"eating jet lag"*; this, too, has been linked to increased body weight[158]. As much as possible, it is beneficial to keep eating and sleeping windows consistent between weekdays and weekends.

The amount of sleep we get can also substantially impact our metabolism. Specifically, chronic sleep loss impairs glucose tolerance and increases the risk of diabetes[44]. Like with sleep and pain, a bidirectional relationship has been found between sleep and obesity; sleep loss can increase the risk of obesity, and obesity can lead to sleep disturbances and sleep loss[44].

The impact of sleep duration on obesity, often measured by body mass index, is thought to be at least partly due to its known influence on appetite regulation. Just like with circadian desynchronisation, sleep deprivation decreases leptin levels and increases ghrelin levels, leading to increases in appetite[44]. Overall, the National Sleep Foundation recommendation of seven to nine hrs of sleep per night[159] is a great first step towards good metabolic health.

Scientific insight: snacking is better than a large meal

In 2019, Charlotte Gupta and friends ran a study to determine how meal timing affects alertness and safety during a night shift. The participants recruited for the study were divided into three groups: those who had a main meal on the night shift, those who had a snack, and those who did not eat. Compared to those who ate a full meal and those who did not eat at all, those who had a snack performed better on reaction time and memory tasks and spent less time speeding and veering out of the correct lane within a simulated driving test[160]. The results of this study suggest that having small snacks regularly (a *grazing* strategy) is the best eating strategy while on the night shift.

6.9   Practical application for nutrition and shiftwork

- If you are working the night shift and plan on having a large meal, consider having it before the start of the shift or within the early stages of the shift (i.e. before midnight)

- Whilst at work, opt for small snacks across the shift that do not exceed 600 calories

- Stay hydrated while on the night shift

- When you finish your night shift, eat before bed, as hunger may wake you up. However, be sure not to have coffee or other caffeinated drinks with this meal

Myth: You may have heard or read on the internet that *"banana peel"* tea helps with sleep. Whilst the articles may state that banana peel tea will help you sleep, it may not. The proposed mechanism behind banana peel tea is that the peel contains some elements that may help, including magnesium. There is little research to endorse the use of banana peel tea to support tea, and we could not find any scientific studies to support these claims.

Want to know more about nutrition and sleep? **?**

Check out Dr Charlotte Gupta's Keynote Presentation, "A Time to Rest, A Time to Dine: Exploring the Link between Nutrition and Sleep for Health and Performance."

Cardiovascular disease poses a serious health and economic burden and is the leading cause of death globally. Two critical modifiable lifestyle factors known to influence cardiovascular health are diet and sleep. These lifestyle factors have been typically investigated independently in science. Here, Dr Gupta introduces the field of chrononutrition, which explores food timing and human circadian rhythm. Through a series of laboratory and field studies findings, Dr Gupta argues that sleep and eating behaviours influence one another and thus should be considered together in any intervention for health and performance.

LISTEN HERE:

https://youtu.be/9mdkhP5GV_U

OR SCAN QR CODE

6.10   Does cannabis help me sleep?

Many people will swear by the positive effects of smoking a "joint" before going to sleep. They will tell you it helps with sleep and helps them relax, and if they don't have it, they sleep poorly and have terrible nightmares. With the relaxation of laws regarding the medicinal and recreational use of marijuana, some people are even saying that their doctors are prescribing "a bag of weed" to them. We are not sure if we have heard of that on a prescription pad (well, at least not in Australia!).

Marijuana

Before we delve into this question, let's explain a few things. There are two main chemical substances within cannabis that produce effects on our body (called cannabinoids) that we focus on (though there are hundreds in cannabis!). These are Δ9-tetrahydrocannabinol (THC) and cannabidiol (CBD).

- THC is the substance that is mainly responsible for the intoxicating, psychoactive "high" that can come with cannabis

- CBD is associated with the relaxation, sedation, and sometimes "therapeutic" effects

Scientific insight: a review of the evidence on cannabis

Alexandra Garcia and Ihsan Salloum completed a review of the scientific research in 2015, looking at how nicotine, caffeine, alcohol, cocaine, opiates and cannabis all impact human sleep [138]. Through their research, they found that acute use (i.e. once off) of cannabis that is low in THC can result in a lower sleep onset latency (taking less time to fall asleep), a larger total sleep time, and more time spent in deep sleep (that stage of sleep that is important for physical repair and growth). However, it also results in less time spent in REM sleep (which is important for brain functioning and is the stage of sleep where most of our dreaming occurs). With higher THC doses, deep sleep appears to decrease with REM sleep, while the time taken to fall asleep increases. One study suggested that longer-term cannabis use results in a decrease in deep sleep, and withdrawal from cannabis use results in individuals taking longer to get to sleep, having less sleep, and spending more of the night awake, though also having an increase in REM sleep; this could explain why some people report having more dreams, which tend to be more vivid (and are often reported as nightmares). However, it does need to be stressed that much of the research in this space is quite limited and hasn't always accounted for all variables [161], so don't be too surprised if the scientific understanding of sleep and cannabis changes as more high-quality studies are conducted.

6.11   Cannabis, sleep disorders and nightmares

There are some studies showing the potential benefits of medicinal (and sometimes synthetic) cannabis for some sleep disorders, including insomnia, OSA, narcolepsy and PTSD-related nightmares [161]. One clinical trial on people with insomnia found the use of a medicinal cannabis substance to improve subjective insomnia symptoms (how the individuals felt about their insomnia), as well as some objective sleep measures (how the individuals actually slept) [162]. We do stress, however, that these clinical trials are using highly controlled medicinal cannabis substances with specific ratios of THC and CBD, there are very often adverse outcomes reported in these studies, and there is currently not enough evidence to support cannabis as a sleep treatment for any sleep issues[161]. Combining all this with the evidence out there that long-term cannabis use and withdrawal symptoms can negatively impact sleep (not to mention the effects it can have on next-day functioning!), we do not advocate for cannabis use for sleep purposes in any way.

Want to know more about cannabis and its potential for treating insomnia? ❓

Sleep4Performance Podcast Season 7 Episode 1: Medical Cannabis and the Benefit to Insomnia with Dr Jen Walsh

LISTEN HERE:

https://sleep4performance.com/podcast/s7-ep1-medical-cannabis-and-the-benefit-to-insomnia/

OR SCAN QR CODE

6.12   Sleep and immunity

Studies have shown that sleeping for less than six hours per night can actually increase the chances of getting the common cold, reduce immune responses (our body's way of fighting illness), and can even reduce the efficacy of certain immunisations[163]. On the other hand, achieving seven or more hours of sleep can improve the immune system's performance[164]. Daily sleep duration can influence the ability to resist infection. Shorter sleep at night has been shown to increase the chances of getting a cold[165] by almost three times compared to those who sleep for seven to nine hours. However, it is essential to remember that other health behaviours beyond sleep are also crucial for our immune systems[166], and should not be neglected even when you are sleeping well!

Regarding sleep and the effectiveness of immunisations, a study looking at Hepatitis B immunisation found that those sleeping less than 6 hrs a night (around the time of immunisation) produced lower antibodies in response to the immunisation when compared to those sleeping for seven or more hrs per night[167]. The shorter sleeping group also showed lower immunity levels, measured both six months and one year after the immunisations.

6.13   Is having a cold shower or ice bath beneficial before sleeping?

Many people who work or exercise in extreme temperatures wish to use cold water immersion to help reduce their heart rate, lower their core body temperature and help them relax. This could include those working in the Western Australia mining industry, those who run in Ultramarathons such as the Badwater 135 in California or those working in smelters or power stations where radiant heat is an issue. In these environments, thermal stress is experienced for prolonged periods, which can result in fatigue.

6.14   Practical application for cold water immersion

- Exposure to cold water may depend on individual preferences, time of year, time of day, and type of activity

- You should slowly adjust your exposure to cold water and monitor its impact on your sleep (either self-reported or via a wearable device)

- Coupling activities (such as swimming, freediving or breathwork) with cold-water immersion may be dangerous. Ensure you always have a buddy with you and keep safe

- Cold water exposure may be best the day after activity instead of post-exercise before bed. Some evidence suggests that cold water immersion immediately after exercise may negatively impact muscle growth (hypertrophy) and physiological adaptation

- Cold water immersion before sleep does not negatively impact your sleep

> ### Scientific insight: cold water does not impact sleep
>
> Research on cold-water exposure or showers has been mainly conducted on athletes. Many athletes use cold water immersion (bathtubs, plunge pools, rivers, lakes, ocean) to facilitate next-day recovery after an event, competition or strenuous activity. Cold water generally reduces inflammation and has been shown by some to support muscular and physical recovery. However, there is very little actual research on how cold water impacts sleep, and the little that has been done has reported inconsistent findings. One study had well-trained endurance runners use 10 mins of cold water prior to bed and found a decrease in nighttime movement and an increase in deep sleep within the early parts of the night [168].

6.15 Supplements for sleep

Many people look for solutions that may not require a medical practitioner's intervention to support them in sleeping. Often, these people turn to supplements. But can they help with sleep? In the next couple of sections, we will discuss two of the most researched supplements for sleep: magnesium and iron.

6.16 Iron supplementation for limb movement disorders

Using meta-analytic techniques (statistically reviewing all research performed in a thorough manner), researchers have reported that iron supplementation is associated with decreased symptoms and can be considered as a safe and effective treatment modality for many individuals with restless leg syndrome [170].

6.17 Does sleep medication help my sleep?

Sometimes, it's just difficult to sleep when working shiftwork or going through irregular work hrs for a project or operational reasons. During these times, people often turn to sleep medications. Prescription hypnotics such as

Scientific insight: magnesium does not directly impact sleep

Magnesium is an essential mineral that supports recovery, reduces muscle cramps and may help with sleep. We can find magnesium in numerous foods, including dairy, soy, nuts, and leafy greens. A recent scientific literature review by Arman Arab and friends, focusing on the role of magnesium in sleep health, found that many of the studies reporting the benefits of magnesium supplementation only consider subjective sleep measures. Additionally, they found that in studies comparing magnesium to a placebo, there is no benefit in magnesium use for sleep [169]. Overall, the evidence for magnesium is not conclusive, and current research suggests that it may not help with sleep.

Some shiftworkers or physically active people swear by the benefits of magnesium. The benefits received may not be directly related to sleep but may have more to do with supplementation aiding recovery by reducing cramps, leg movements, aches, and pains, all of which are important to manage before sleep. Additionally, there are no adverse effects of taking magnesium within recommended doses. So, if you find magnesium to be beneficial for you personally, there is no reason not to use it! We note that magnesium is best taken after food, e.g., after dinner/within 2 hrs of sleep.

WARNING: If you take magnesium on an empty stomach, it may cause diarrhea and cramping in the stomach.

temazepam, zolpidem, eszopiclone, and zaleplon have been shown to help induce and maintain sleep, even when the circumstances or environment around the sleep are not optimal. Given that sleep loss is a significant risk factor in safety and performance, it is logical to expect that even an artificial sleep period is better than no sleep, poor sleep, or too little sleep.

When it comes to deciding which sleep medication is appropriate, the timing of sleep opportunity and the potential for needing to be up and alert earlier than expected are important considerations. A good example of this is on-call work; taking sleep medication which causes significant drowsiness if awake during the night is obviously a poor choice for on-call workers. We encourage sleep medication use to occur only with consultation from a medical professional (i.e. your GP) and with disclosure of use within any relevant medication notification documentation within your workplace.

Importantly, we want to stress that medication is not a long-term solution for sleep problems and is only a temporary fix while the underlying issue (stress, insomnia, or the presence of a sleep disorder) is addressed. If you experience sleep problems for more than two weeks while taking sleep medication, we strongly recommend seeking additional advice.

6.18 How does electronic device use impact sleep?

Electronic device use is ever-increasing in the general population[171]. Many people use electronic devices for social media, communicating with family and friends, working, listening to music, and watching movies. The popular media often discusses how electronic devices used late in the evening can negatively impact sleep (particularly for teenagers). However, you may be surprised to learn that the extent to which electronic devices affect sleep and how this impact occurs is still hotly debated by scientists today!

Laptop Use Late At Night

There are **three proposed** ways that electronic device use may impact nighttime sleep:

1. **Artificial light** emitted from electronic devices (or other artificial sources) is often "blue-enriched", meaning it is a particular spectrum of light that our body and circadian rhythm is particularly sensitive to. Studies have shown that even small amounts of light from artificial sources such as a smartphone can greatly interfere with natural melatonin (the hormone that signals that it is nighttime) release within our body[172,173], and that this impact is highly variable between people[174]. Some studies show that this can lead to an increase in sleep onset latency[175] (it takes longer to fall asleep) and a reduction in deep sleep[176]; however, summaries or *meta-analyses* have shown that these effects are small and non-consistent[177, 178].

2. Electronic devices are often used for **activities that are either cognitively stimulating or potentially stressful**. An example of a cognitively stimulating activity could be playing a competitive action video game, while a "stressful" activity could be checking work emails or share prices. Practically, this suggests that there is a difference between watching junk TV prior to bed and playing a shooter video game prior to bed. However, provided the activity doesn't keep the individual from going to bed, studies so far have suggested that the impact of "content" is relatively small[179, 180].

3. People may be **engaging with their electronic device in place of sleep**. This is extremely common – an individual may decide that they want to go to bed at 10:00 PM but find that they are still scrolling through social media on their phone at 10:30 PM. Obviously, that individual has then lost 30 min of sleep opportunity. From the research that has been performed so far, this *appears* to be the main way electronic devices impact sleep in the real world[178]. Thinking in this way, using electronic devices at night becomes a game of discipline:

   "Will I actually stop using the device at my normal bedtime?"

   "Will I refrain from reaching for my phone if I am struggling to sleep?"

This is one of the main reasons that we recommend avoiding work-related activities (i.e. emails) on our devices within 2 hrs of bedtime and switching to less engaging and more relaxing activities in the hour before bed: it will make sure we aren't staying up to watch one more episode or to send one more email. We also note that social media (i.e. Facebook, Instagram, X, and LinkedIn) are specifically designed to keep you engaged and use time spent on the platform as a measure of success. Therefore, we recommend avoiding social media use at least 30 mins before bedtime, to avoid falling into their traps.

6.19 Practical application for the use of electronic devices

Avoid stimulating activities such as work-related emails or tasks at least 2 hrs before bed and substitute the type of content you watch in the 1 hr before sleep for more relaxing activities. Avoid social media ideally 1 hr before sleep and within 30 mins of sleep. Most importantly, make sure that you are not sacrificing sleep time to watch one more episode or send one more email, and avoid using your electronic device if you are struggling to fall asleep.

6.20 How do I control the sleep environment?

The environment in which we relax, and sleep can considerably impact the quantity and quality of sleep we get each night. Environmental factors that may affect sleep include noise, light, temperature, and the comfort of a bed/pillow. Routine (e.g., having the same room, familiarity with the environment, going to bed and waking up at a similar time) also has an effect. This is often referred to as sleep hygiene or good sleep habits. The home sleep environment should be a sanctuary where we relax and recuperate; this is why we usually state in sleep science that the bedroom should only be for sleep and sex.

An easy way to imagine an ideal sleep environment is that humans like to sleep in caves; caves are cool, dark, and quiet. These are the three major properties of an ideal sleep environment.

Figure 21. Your sleep environment should be like a cave: cool, dark, and quiet...can you find something similar!

When we travel, we often change our sleeping environments regularly. The quality of the sleeping environment may vary, as will the additional factors such as noise and light. The following items should be considered when changing sleeping environments to maximise sleep and recovery.

6.21 Practical application for setting up your sleep environment

- Are the windows blacked out? Can any visible light be seen through the windows with all doors closed? If visible lights show through windows, use opaque materials (e.g. aluminium foil and tape) to blacken

- When placing aluminium foil over a window, cut out a piece that exactly fits the windowpane. Then, wet one side of the aluminium foil and place the wet side over the window. This allows the aluminium foil to maintain a perfect seal with the windowpane and will not make noise if a fan or air conditioner is blowing in the room. When travelling, always bring an eye mask, just in case

- Are there any sources of distracting light (e.g. mobile phones, digital clocks/radios, and standby lights from electrical equipment)?

- Tape over/turn off standby lights, direct light from the phone, and put digital clock/radios away from view

- Is the air conditioner set between 18°C and 24°C (ideally 21°C)? Is the air conditioner on a maintenance schedule to ensure correct functioning (i.e. right temperature, low noise/no vibration of motors)?

- If you cannot control the temperature, is there access to a fan for cooling, or can you get extra blankets for heating?

- Is the room insulated from external noise to allow quality sleep? Are there external building noise barriers (e.g. high fence)?

- Are there controls to minimise noise from other sources in the room (e.g. vibration from fridge motors)?

- Consider the use of earplugs to reduce noise whilst sleeping

6.22 Why do I not sleep well in a hotel (or unfamiliar environment), and can I avoid this phenomenon?

Hotels provide a sleep space, a home away from home. Despite this, many people struggle to fall asleep or get good quality sleep in hotels. A study showed that, on average, individuals slept less in hotels than at home[181]. So, is there something that we can do to get better sleep when sleeping in a hotel?

Researchers have explored three categories of factors that can lead to sleep difficulties when sleeping in hotels: personal, hotel, and travel-related factors[182, 183].

- Personal factors include, for instance, the purpose of the stay. Travelling for business can be highly stressful and is linked to sleep difficulties. Even when travelling for pleasure, trying to fit in many experiences in a short time window can be stressful

- Common hotel factors include uncomfortable bed linen, uncomfortable pillows, and sound from the air conditioning or heater[184]. Further, noise from streets, poor indoor climate, sunlight coming through the window, noise from the ventilation system, poor mattress, and high room temperature can also negatively impact sleep[181]

- Travel factors include any lingering effects of jet lag and/or travel fatigue that may be experienced when sleeping in a hotel at the destination location

6.23 Practical application for staying in a hotel

Although many factors can impact your sleep in a hotel, there are some tips you can follow to get better sleep when staying in a hotel.

Plan wisely: Whilst we always want to maximise the experience of our short stays, be mindful of your sleep. Maybe don't have a late night upon arrival. Maybe have a sleep-in. It may also be worth adjusting to the destination time before the travel to reduce the effect of jet lag.

- **Do your homework:** When booking a hotel, a few factors must be considered. Reading the hotel reviews is always a recommended first step. For instance, do people complain about noisy cleaning staff in the morning?

- **Consider the hotel location.** Is the hotel located on a busy street with many restaurants? This may result in noise late at night. If it is not explicitly stated in the hotel description, ask whether temperature control (e.g., air conditioning) and block-out curtains are available

- **Request a room away from elevators**, ice machines, and other noisy areas. Rooms on higher floors may have less street noise. It may be worth spending slightly more on a better hotel if that means better sleep

- **Inspect your hotel room**: When you arrive at your hotel room, identify potential sources of sleep disruptors. For instance, is the fridge or air conditioning too noisy? Or does your window face a streetlight, and the curtains may not block out all the light at night? Speak to the hotel manager and request a different room

- **Arrive prepared:** If there is light or noise you cannot eliminate, always travel with earplugs and an eye mask. They are small and light and fit into every suitcase or bag. It may even be beneficial to travel with your pillow

Interesting: Research has shown that guests who were more satisfied with their sleep during their stay rated the hotel better[184].

6.24 Why do I sleep better away from home than at home?

While uncommon, some people have described that they struggle to sleep well in their own bed and sleep better in other environments such as a hotel. Why may that be? To date, no scientific study has investigated this phenomenon. However, a few assumptions can be made based on the factors we know can impact sleep.

One of these factors could be having children at home, particularly young kids, which can result in waking up during the night. Furthermore, your children's or partners' schedules may not align with yours. When sleeping at home, early morning or late evening commitments can result in irregular sleep timing (e.g., going to bed and waking up at different times from day to day), disrupting our internal body clock and impairing our sleep[185]. Sleeping with another person in the same bedroom can compromise the sleep environment setup due to different individual preferences. This can include, for instance, the air temperature and the bedding. Additionally, a bed partner can disrupt our sleep by moving in bed, getting up to use the toilet, snoring, or pulling the blanket away [186,187]. Having pets in the bedroom can also disrupt our sleep, as they move around and can be noisy at night[188]. In addition, animals have different sleep patterns than humans[189]. These are just some examples of the many factors that can disturb sleep at home.

6.25 Practical applications for the sleep environment

- If your sleep is disturbed at home, identifying the causes is incredibly important. Take some time to think of what factors are leading you to have a disturbed sleep

- If you share your sleeping environment with a bed partner, settle on a room temperature that works best for both of you. If one person prefers a lower temperature, having the room at that lower temperature and the other bed partner using an extra blanket may be the way to go

- Along similar lines, consider what types of mattresses are most conducive to sleep for you and your bed partner. If these answers are different between the two of you, consider using two separate single mattresses

- Choose a pillow that is most comfortable for you

- Keeping your pets out of your bedroom may help you to sleep through

- When returning from the site, consider sleeping in a separate room during the first few nights to avoid being interrupted by your partner or children

- Speak to your partner about the importance of prioritising sleep when returning home from your time on-site

- Aim for regular bedtimes and wake-up times when you're at home. This will help you fall asleep quicker and stay asleep through the night

6.26 What is the best pillow or mattress for sleep?

We have all walked down the road and seen a sign about how a bed or a mattress will scientifically make you sleep better. You walk into the store and peruse the variety of beds and mattresses. The salesperson asks about your needs, use, and budget and may direct you to the latest sleep technology mattress or other variation. But what exactly is the scientific evidence? Do these bed mattresses make you sleep better?

If you go to PubMed (a database of peer-reviewed scientific literature) and enter the search terms "Sleep and Mattress", you will find over 900 studies. However, you might be surprised to know that while many studies have looked at different mattresses and pain (often back pain), less than five of these studies are exploring how mattresses positively or negatively impact sleep! So, what do these studies looking at mattresses and sleep say?

6.27 What research is out there on mattresses and their impact on sleep?

A 2020 study conducted in France explored how a "high-heat capacity mattress" could potentially improve the post-match sleep of elite rugby players. This mattress was specially designed to remove transfer heat away from the body, reducing the likelihood of running too hot during a night's sleep. The researchers found that when players used the mattress, there was a very small decrease in their nighttime period awake and an increase in the proportion of their sleep being in REM sleep, but no other changes to the athlete's sleep[190].

Going a level up from mattresses (literally), a couple of studies have explored how different mattress toppers can impact sleep outcomes. One study compared low-rebound (pressure-absorbing/memory foam) and

high-rebound mattress toppers and observed the impact on sleep. For reference, "memory foam" products would be considered low-rebound, and a firmer resin & fibre-based mattress or topper would be considered high-rebound. The researchers found that using a high-rebound topper in the first half of the night resulted in a lower body temperature and deeper sleep. However, a subsequent study found no difference between the two mattress types regarding sleep measures for young male athletes.

Scientific insight: novel mattress designs

One research group in Sweden explored the impact of a mattress specifically designed to promote prone sleeping (sleeping on your front) [192]. This mattress was developed specifically for people with OSA (particularly those who cannot tolerate CPAP or only use their machine periodically [193]), as sleeping prone can significantly reduce the impact of OSA on a night's sleep when compared to sleeping on their back. The study found that when people with OSA slept on the specially designed mattress, they spent more time sleeping on their front, and markers of OSA severity dropped by 50%. Another research team in the United States studied a mattress that vibrates and creates sound throughout the night, which was specially designed for children with autism spectrum disorder (ASD). The group found it to increase both the amount of sleep obtained and the quality of sleep as well in this population [190].

However, they did find that athletes who slept on high-rebound toppers for four to six weeks actually ran faster afterwards [191].

6.28 Do weighted blankets help with sleep?

Weighted blankets are a non-pharmacological alternative sleep aid [194]. The concept of weighted blankets is simple; they provide gentle and evenly distributed pressure (deep touch pressure), which relaxes the nervous system. Like receiving a hug, weighted blankets' deep touch pressure increases serotonin and melatonin levels while decreasing cortisol. Through this mechanism, studies have shown benefits for the use of weighted blankets for (but not limited to) anxiety/ distress levels of inpatients at psychiatric facilities [195,196], residents [197] in nursing homes, and adult patients recovering from chemotherapy, [198] as well as a reduction of symptoms for infants with Neonatal Abstinence Syndrome [199].

Just like the sound and vibration-producing mattress, weighted blankets have received much attention as a potential aid in mitigating sleep problems in children with ASD. Consistent sensory stimulation from the weighted blanket has been said to promote sleep for children with ASD.

However, while children and parents have reported favourable things about the blankets, studies have shown a minimal[200] or no[201] change in measured objective sleep outcomes (how the child actually slept). Another study looked at the potential of weighted blankets for children with attention-deficit/hyperactivity disorder (ADHD) and again found that parents reported positive things regarding their impact on sleep and daily life [202]. However, this study did not take any objective sleep measures, so we cannot say for sure that sleep improved.

For adults, little science has explored whether weighted blankets can improve sleep. Promisingly, one study by members of SleepScore Labs found that for adults with issues getting or falling asleep, using a weighted blanket reduced the amount of time awake during a nighttime period and reduced the proportion of "light sleep" within a night sleep[203]. Weighted blanket users also self-reported being less stressed at bedtime, falling asleep quicker, having better quality sleep, and feeling refreshed. Another study found that weighted blanket use reduced chronic pain in suffering adults; however, it produced no objective benefit in sleep outcomes[204]. Besides these two studies, there is nothing else in the peer-reviewed literature on whether weighted blanket use benefits adults' sleep. It is tough to recommend weighted blankets for sleep, given the lack of evidence out there, and the fact that the evidence out there is quite mixed. Weighted blankets are safe and feasible for populations provided the correct blanket weight (typically 10% of body weight); the only real issue with weighted blankets is that they can get too hot for some people. Hence, if you are intrigued and want to see if a weighted blanket suits you, go for it; just do not expect any sleep miracles.

6.29 How does environmental noise affect sleep?

Noise at bedtime seems like a straightforward factor to control on the surface, however many people experience noise-related sleep disturbances every day. Noise impacting sleep is such an issue that the

Scientific insight: Noisy neighbourhoods cause sleep problems

In a study at the Walter Reed Army Institute of Research in the United States they recruited over 2,000 adults who were from randomly selected Chicago, Miami, Bronx, and San Diego households. The researchers had these adults wear validated sleep-tracking wristwatches. Nearly half of individuals reported violence and noise as neighbourhood problems, and almost a quarter considered their neighbourhood unsafe. This was then found to be linked to getting less sleep and poorer quality sleep, as well as higher rates of insomnia [207].

Scientific insight: Noisy rail causes sleep problems

While not everyone may have a noisy neighbourhood due to crime or shouting, this research's results apply to those who live near main roads, freeways or highways that may have much traffic during periods of sleep. While governments will often aim to install noise reduction systems through vegetation, infrastructure, use of speed limits, and the limited use of air brakes, these measures are frequently insufficient. Similar issues arise when people live near airports, train lines, and bus stations.

A study from a research group in Germany in 2006 showed the impact of noise emitted from road, rail and air traffic and its effect on sleep. The research team recruited 32 people (16 men and 16 women) who spent 21 consecutive nights in a laboratory. Eight people slept in a quiet environment throughout, while the remaining 24 had to sleep among road, rail or aircraft noises of variable noise levels. The researchers found that sleep quality and cognitive performance (tested in the morning) both worsened with increasing nighttime noise levels, with rail noise resulting in the worst sleep out of all noises [208].

In 2022, a study in Denmark found road traffic noise to be associated with an increased risk of various undesirable health conditions, such as ischemic heart disease, myocardial infarction, angina pectoris, and heart failure [209]. Specifically for heart disease, sleep disturbances were reported as a potential reason for this increased risk. Stress leading to increased cortisol levels could also help explain some of the increased risk; in a study with 439 people in six European countries had their cortisol levels assessed three times a day (morning, lunch, and evening) using saliva samples. They found a significant increase in cortisol levels in the morning in females after exposure to aircraft noise [210].

World Health Organization (WHO) has sleep disturbances down as one of the seven adverse health and social effects of noise pollution [205].

Nocturnal environmental noise can increase cortisol, adrenaline, heart rate, and even blood pressure [206]. Studies have shown that noise within a neighbourhood can profoundly impact the quality of our sleep. Certain suburbs within the United States with higher-than-average crime rates have more significant noise-related sleep disturbances [207]. This is due to more regular noise at night, such as shouting, gunshots, and the sirens of emergency vehicles passing through.

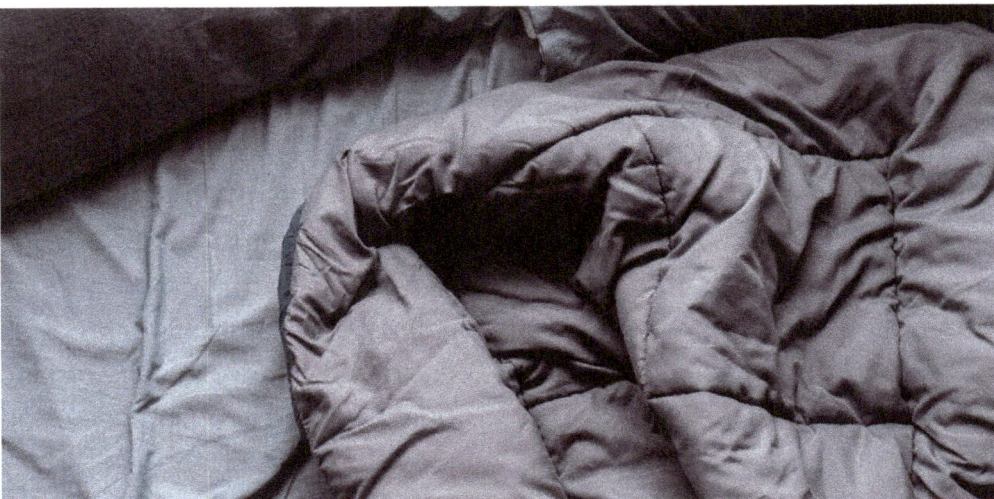

6.30 Practical application for noise reduction

- Consider installing sound-reduction walls in your sleep environment. Double glazing will also help
- Consider specific noise-reduction techniques, such as earplugs and noise-cancelling headphones. These technologies have developed rapidly over the years, and many devices are available on the market

6.31 Can lavender oils and other scents improve my ability to fall asleep?

Aromatherapy is an alternative therapy that involves applying essential oils, such as lavender oil, through inhalation or massage. This therapy is famous for its relaxing effect. Some believe essential oils improve sleep, but does the evidence support this belief?

Unfortunately, very little quality research has been performed exploring the effectiveness of essential oils, such as lavender oil, for better sleep[211]. Additionally, studies conducted have tended to consider self-reported sleep outcomes rather than exploring whether this therapy *actually* impacts sleep[212,213]. The good news is that the application of essential oils is considered safe, with a low risk of side effects[211]. Therefore, there is no harm in trying essential oils to see if they personally provide you with any benefit.

If you are curious and new to applying essential oils, there are a few points to consider. Firstly, different oils smell different, and not everyone finds all essential oils pleasant; use a little trial and error and settle on an essential oil you like the smell of. Secondly, consider the odour intensity; too strong, and it could lead to headaches instead of relaxation. Consider the size of your bedroom and whether you sleep with the door/window open or closed; you may need one small product, or multiple products. The product's location should also be considered; if you place the product on the bedside table, its proximity to you could lead to an intense odour, even if only one product is used.

Interesting: There are more than 200 species of Lavender, with Lavandula angustifolia being the most used species for lavender oil. Lavender oil is produced by steam-distilling the flowering heads.

7. Final Thoughts

Managing sleep health in shift work environments is a complex challenge. While there are many excellent books on general sleep science and information, we noticed a gap when it comes to specific guidance for shift workers and those with irregular schedules. This book aimed to fill that gap by providing up-to-date scientific information and practical advice tailored to optimising recovery and performance, whether you're interested in general sleep health or specifically in managing shift work.

This book serves as a valuable reference for shift workers, those designing shifts and rosters, and those developing or implementing fatigue risk management systems. It is also a useful resource for leaders, managers, shift supervisors, and the families of shift workers, helping them gain a broader understanding of sleep management.

We hope you found some valuable insights into safely managing shift work, improving sleep, and enhancing daily performance. We will continue to keep this book up to date as new scientific and evidence-based research and solutions arise. For other aspects of sleep and fatigue, such as designing fatigue management systems, scientifically developing shifts and rosters, the importance of sleep for athletic performance and more, be sure to connect with us at Melius Consulting or Sleep4Performance.

Sleep Well!!!

8. Courses and Education

At Melius Consulting, we offer a variety of guest educational talks on sleep and athletic performance, dreams and nightmares, women's health and much more. If you enjoyed this book, you may like our Sleep Health and Fatigue Management Education Sessions

Melius Consulting is your trusted source for Sleep Health and Fatigue Education. Our consultants are seasoned scientific experts in sleep science, chronobiology, fatigue management and fitness for work. We provide a comprehensive course including sleep science, chronobiology, sleep problems and disorders, the impact of fatigue and poor sleep, vehicles and driving and optimising shiftwork.

Participants will gain invaluable insights into managing shiftwork, improve their understanding of fatigue's impact, and learn how to optimise their sleep and performance.

The knowledge transferred in this course isn't confined to the workplace; it integrates into all aspects of life, work-life balance, family, and enhancing physical and cognitive performance.

Benefits include:

- Optimised workforce wellness

- Reduced incidents and accidents

- Enhanced employee engagement

Our engaging courses are conducted within a ~3.5 hour timeframe and are tailored to accommodate your business and team's needs.

You can choose between face-to-face sessions or the convenience of online delivery via Microsoft Teams, accommodating groups of up to 25 individuals.

9. References

1. Palca JW, Walker JM, Berger RJ. Thermoregulation, metabolism, and stages of sleep in cold-exposed men. *Journal of Applied Physiology*. Sep 1986;61(3):940-947. https://doi.org/10.1152/jappl.1986.61.3.940

2. Haskell EH, Palca JW, Walker JM, Berger RJ, Heller HC. The effects of high and low ambient temperatures on human sleep stages. *Electroencephalography and Clinical Neurophysiology*. May 1981;51(5):494-501. https://doi.org/10.1016/0013-4694(81)90226-1

3. Crispim CA, Padilha HG, Zimberg IZ, et al. Adipokine Levels Are Altered by Shiftwork: A Preliminary Study. *Chronobiology International*. Jun 2012;29(5):587-594. https://10.3109/07420528.2012.675847

4. Reilly T, Edwards B. Altered sleep–wake cycles and physical performance in athletes. *Physiology & Behavior*. Feb 2007;90(2–3):274-284. https://doi.org/10.1016/j.physbeh.2006.09.017

5. Gupta L, Morgan K, Gilchrist S. Does Elite Sport Degrade Sleep Quality? A Systematic Review. *Sports Medicine*. Nov 2016; 47:1317-1333. https://doi:10.1007/s40279-016-0650-6

6. Van Dongen HP, Maislin G, Mullington JM, Dinges DF. The cumulative cost of additional wakefulness: dose-response effects on neurobehavioral functions and sleep physiology from chronic sleep restriction and total sleep deprivation. *Sleep*. Mar 2003;26(2):117-126. https://doi.org/10.1093/sleep/26.2.117

7. Dinges DF, Pack F, Williams K, et al. Cumulative sleepiness, mood disturbance, and psychomotor vigilance performance decrements during a week of sleep restricted to 4-5 hours per night. *Sleep*. Apr 1997;20(4):267-277. https://doi.org/10.1093/sleep/20.4.267

8. Durmer JS, Dinges DF. Neurocognitive consequences of sleep deprivation. *Seminars in Neurology*. 2005;25(1):117-129. https://doi.org/ 10.1055/s-2005-867080

9. Barbera J. Sleep and dreaming in Greek and Roman philosophy. *Sleep Medicine*. Dec 2008;9(8):906-910. https://doi.org/10.1016/j.sleep.2007.10.010

10. Zordan M, Costa R, Macino G, Fukuhara C, Tosini G. Circadian Clocks: What Makes Them Tick?. *Chronobiology International*. 2000;17(4):433-451. https://doi.org/10.1081/CBI-100101056

11. Helden AV. The Galileo Project. Accessed 20/11/2017. http://galileo.rice.edu/Catalog/NewFiles/mairan.html

12. Pelayo R, Dement WC. Chapter 1 - History of Sleep Physiology and Medicine. In: Kryger M, Roth T, Dement WC, eds. *Principles and Practice of Sleep Medicine (Sixth Edition)*. Elsevier; 2017:3-14.

13. Todman D. History of Sleep Medicine *The Internet Journal of Neurology*. 2007;9(2). http://galileo.rice.edu/Catalog/NewFiles/mairan.html

14. Dement WC, Vaughan, C. *The promise of sleep: a pioneer in sleep medicine explains the vital connection between health, happiness, and a good night's sleep.* Dell Publishing Co;1999.

15. Lavie P. *The Enchanted World of Sleep.* Yale University Press; 1997.

16. Deloitte Access Economics. *Asleep on the job: costs of inadequate sleep in Australia.* Sleep Health Foundation; Aug 2017. Accessed 07/10/2024. https://www.sleephealthfoundation.org.au/special-sleep-reports/asleep-on-the-job-costs-of-inadequate-sleep-in-australia

17. Ohayon M, Wickwire EM, Hirshkowitz M, et al. National Sleep Foundation's sleep quality recommendations: first report. *Sleep Health.* Feb 2017;3(1):6-19. https://doi.org/10.1016/j.sleh.2016.11.006

18. Cribb L, Sha R, Yiallourou S, et al. Sleep Regularity and Mortality: A Prospective Analysis in the UK Biobank. *eLife.* Nov 2023;12:RP88359. https://doi.org/10.7554/eLife.88359.3

19. Winget CM, DeRoshia CW, Holley DC. Circadian Rhythms and Athletic Performance *Medicine and science in sports and exercise.* Oct 1985;17(5):498-516.

20. van Oosterhout F, Lucassen EA, Houben T, vanderLeest HT, Antle MC, Meijer JH. Amplitude of the SCN Clock Enhanced by the Behavioral Activity Rhythm. *PLoS One.* Jun 2012;7(6)e39693. https://doi.org/10.1371/journal.pone.0039693

21. Edwards S, Evans P, Hucklebridge F, Clow A. Association between time of awakening and diurnal cortisol secretory activity. *Psychoneuroendocrinology.* Aug 2001;26(6):613-622. https://doi.org/10.1016/s0306-4530(01)00015-4

22. Burgess HJ, Trinder J, Kim Y, Luke D. Sleep and circadian influences on cardiac autonomic nervous system activity. *The American Journal of Physiology.* Oct 1997;273(4):H1761-1768. https://doi.org/10.1152/ajpheart.1997.273.4.H1761

23. Duffy JF, Czeisler CA. Effect of Light on Human Circadian Physiology. *Sleep Medicine Clinics.* Jun 2009;4(2):165-177. https://doi.org/10.1016/j.jsmc.2009.01.004

24. Diaz MM, Bocanegra OL, Teixeira RR, Tavares M, Soares SS, Espindola FS. The Relationship Between The Cortisol Awakening Response, Mood States and Performance. *Journal of Strength and Conditioning Research.* May 2013;27(5):1340-1348. https://doi.org/10.1519/JSC.0b013e318267a612

25. Edwards S, Clow A, Evans P, Hucklebridge F. Exploration of the awakening cortisol response in relation to diurnal cortisol secretory activity. *Life Sciences.* Mar 2001;68(18):2093-2103. https://doi.org/10.1016/s0024-3205(01)00996-1

26. Roenneberg T. *Internal Time: Chronotypes, Social Jet Lag, and Why You're So Tired.* Harvard University Press; 2012.

27. Shekleton JA, Rajaratnam SMW, Gooley JJ, Van Reen E, Czeisler CA, Lockley SW. Improved neurobehavioral performance during the wake maintenance zone. *Journal of Clinical Sleep Medicine.* Apr 2013;9(4):353-362. https://doi.org/10.5664/jcsm.2588

28. Dawson D, Reid K. Fatigue, alcohol and performance impairment. *Nature.* Jul 1997;388(6639):235. https://doi.org/10.1038/40775

29. Samuels C. Sleep, recovery, and performance: the new frontier in high-performance athletics. *Neurologic Clinics*. Feb 2008;26(1):169-180. https://doi.org/10.1016/j.ncl.2007.11.012

30. Dattilo M, Antunes HK, Medeiros A, et al. Sleep and muscle recovery: endocrinological and molecular basis for a new and promising hypothesis. *Medical Hypotheses*. Aug 2011;77(2):220-222. https://doi.org/10.1016/j.mehy.2011.04.017

31. Aisbett B, Condo D, Zacharewicz E, Lamon S. The Impact of Shiftwork on Skeletal Muscle Health. *Nutrients*. Mar 2017;9(3):248. https://doi.org/10.3390/nu9030248

32. Leproult R, Van Cauter E. Role of Sleep and Sleep Loss in Hormonal Release and Metabolism. *Endocrine Development*. Nov 2010;17:11-21. https://doi.org/10.1159/000262524

33. Fischer D, Lombardi DA, Marucci-Wellman H, Roenneberg T. Chronotypes in the US - Influence of age and sex. *PLoS One*. Jun 2017;12(6):e0178782. https://doi.org/10.1371/journal.pone.0178782

34. Zavada A, Gordijn MC, Beersma DG, Daan S, Roenneberg T. Comparison of the Munich Chronotype Questionnaire with the Horne-Ostberg's Morningness-Eveningness Score. *Chronobiology International*. 2005;22(2):267-78. https://doi.org/10.1081/CBI-200053536

35. Islam Z, Hu H, Akter S, et al. Social jetlag is associated with an increased likelihood of having depressive symptoms among the Japanese working population: the Furukawa Nutrition and Health Study. *Sleep*. Jan 13 2020;43(1): zsz204. https://doi.org/10.1093/sleep/zsz204

36. Mitler MM, Carskadon MA, Czeisler CA, Dement WC, Dinges DF, Graeber RC. Catastrophes, sleep, and public policy: consensus report. *Sleep*. Jan 1988;11(1):100-109. https://doi.org/10.1093/sleep/11.1.100

37. Folkard S, Tucker P. Shift work, safety and productivity. *Occupational Medicine*. Mar 2003;53(2):95-101. https://doi.org/10.1093/occmed/kqg047

38. Cho S-S, Lee D-W, Kang M-Y. The Association between Shift Work and Health-Related Productivity Loss due to Either Sickness Absence or Reduced Performance at Work: A Cross-Sectional Study of Korea. *International Journal of Environmental Research and Public Health*. Nov 2020;17(22):8493. https://doi.org/10.3390/ijerph17228493

39. Sateia MJ. International classification of sleep disorders-third edition: highlights and modifications. *Chest*. Nov 2014;146(5):1387-1394. https://doi.org/10.1378/chest.14-0970

40. Fulda S, Schulz H. Cognitive dysfunction in sleep disorders. *Sleep Medicine Reviews*. Dec 2001;5(6):423-445. https://doi.org/10.1053/smrv.2001.0157

41. Bucks R, Olaithe M, Eastwood P. Neurocognitive function in obstructive sleep apnoea: A meta-review. *Respirology*. Jan 2013;18(1):61-70. https://doi.org/10.1111/j.1440-1843.2012.02255.x

42. Fullagar HH, Skorski S, Duffield R, Hammes D, Coutts AJ, Meyer T. Sleep and athletic performance: the effects of sleep loss on exercise performance, and physiological and cognitive responses to exercise. *Sports Medicine*. Feb 2015;45(2):161-186. https://doi.org/10.1007/s40279-014-0260-0

43. Yaggi HK, Concato J, Kernan WN, Lichtman JH, Brass LM, Mohsenin V. Obstructive sleep apnea as a risk factor for stroke and death. *New England Journal of Medicine*. Dec 2005;353(19):2034-2041. https://doi.org/10.1056/NEJMoa043104

44. Van Cauter E, Spiegel K, Tasali E, Leproult R. Metabolic consequences of sleep and sleep loss. *Sleep Medicine*. 2008;9(0 1):S23-S28. https://doi.org/10.1016/S1389-9457(08)70013-3

45. Heinzer R, Vat S, Marques-Vidal P, et al. Prevalence of sleep-disordered breathing in the general population: the HypnoLaus study. *The Lancet Respiratory Medicine*. Apr 2015;3(4):310-318. https://doi.org/10.1016/s2213-2600(15)00043-0

46. Reynolds AC, Appleton SL, Gill TK, Adams RJ. *Chronic Insomnia Disorder in Australia*. Jul 2019. Accessed 07/10/24, https://www.sleephealthfoundation.org.au/special-sleep-reports/chronic-insomnia-disorder-in-australia

47. Kelly JM, Strecker RE, Bianchi MT. Recent developments in home sleep-monitoring devices. *International Scholarly Research Notices*. Oct 2012:768794. https://doi.org/10.5402/2012/768794

48. Standards of Practice Committee of the American Sleep Disorders Association. Practice parameters for the use of polysomnography in the evaluation of insomnia. *Sleep*. Jan 1995;18(1):55-57. https://doi.org/10.1093/sleep/18.1.55

49. Shapiro CM, Bortz R, Mitchell D, Bartel P, Jooste P. Slow-wave sleep: a recovery period after exercise. *Science*. Dec 1981;214(4526):1253-1254. https://doi.org/10.1126/science.7302594

50. Deloitte Access Economics. *Re-awakening Australia – The Economic Cost of Sleep Disorders in Australia*. Oct 2011. Accessed 07/10/2024. https://www.sleephealthfoundation.org.au/pdfs/news/Executive%20summary.pdf

51. Somers VK, White DP, Amin R, et al. Sleep apnea and cardiovascular disease: an American Heart Association/American College of Cardiology Foundation Scientific Statement from the American Heart Association Council for High Blood Pressure Research Professional Education Committee, Council on Clinical Cardiology, Stroke Council, and Council on Cardiovascular Nursing In Collaboration With the National Heart, Lung, and Blood Institute National Center on Sleep Disorders Research (National Institutes of Health). *Journal of the American College of Cardiology*. Aug 2008;52(8):686-717. https://doi.org/10.1016/j.jacc.2008.05.002

52. Marshall NS, Wong KKH, Phillips CL, Liu PY, Knuiman MW, Grunstein RR. Is Sleep Apnea an Independent Risk Factor for Prevalent and Incident Diabetes in the Busselton Health Study? *Journal of Clinical Sleep Medicine*. Feb 2009;5(1):15-20. https://doi.org/10.5664/jcsm.27387

53. Lal C, Strange C, Bachman D. Neurocognitive Impairment in Obstructive Sleep Apnea. *Chest*. Jun 2012;141(6):1601-1610. https://doi.org/10.1378/chest.11-2214

54. Howard ME, Desai AV, Grunstein RR, et al. Sleepiness, sleep-disordered breathing, and accident risk factors in commercial vehicle drivers. *American Journal of Respiratory and Critical Care Medicine*. Nov 2004;170(9):1014-1021. https://doi.org/10.1164/rccm.200312-1782oc

55. Tregear S, Reston J, Schoelles K, Phillips B. Obstructive Sleep Apnea and Risk of Motor Vehicle Crash: Systematic Review and Meta-Analysis. *Journal of Clinical Sleep Medicine*. Dec 2009;5(6):573-581. https://doi.org/10.5664/jcsm.27662

56. Senaratna CV, Perret JL, Lodge CJ, et al. Prevalence of obstructive sleep apnea in the general population: A systematic review. *Sleep Medicine Reviews*. Aug 2017;34:70-81. https://doi.org/10.1016/j.smrv.2016.07.002

57. Rajaratnam SMW, Barger LK, Lockley SW, et al. Sleep Disorders, Health, and Safety in Police Officers. *JAMA*. Dec 2011;306(23):2567-2578. https://doi.org/10.1001/jama.2011.1851

58. Wall H, Smith C, Hubbard R. Body mass index and obstructive sleep apnoea in the UK: a cross-sectional study of the over-50s. *Primary Care Respiratory Journal*. Dec 2012;21(4):371-376. https://doi.org/10.4104/pcrj.2012.00053

59. Andrade FM, Pedrosa RP. The role of physical exercise in obstructive sleep apnea. *Jornal Brasileiro de Pneumologia*. Nov-Dec 2016;42(6):457-464. https://doi.org/10.1590/s1806-37562016000000156

60. Carvalho B, Hsia J, Capasso R. Surgical therapy of obstructive sleep apnea: a review. *Neurotherapeutics*. Oct 2012;9(4):710-716. https://doi.org/10.1007/s13311-012-0141-x

61. Huang T-W, Young T-H. Novel Porous Oral Patches for Patients with Mild Obstructive Sleep Apnea and Mouth Breathing. *Otolaryngology–Head and Neck Surgery*. 2015;152(2):369-373. https://doi.org/10.1177/0194599814559383

62. Jau J-Y, Kuo TBJ, Li LPH, et al. Mouth puffing phenomena of patients with obstructive sleep apnea when mouth-taped: device's efficacy confirmed with physical video observation. *Sleep and Breathing*. Mar 2023;27(1):153-164. https://doi.org/10.1007/s11325-022-02588-0

63. Young T, Peppard PE, Taheri S. Excess weight and sleep-disordered breathing. *Journal of Applied Physiology*. Oct 2005;99(4):1592-1599. https://doi.org/10.1152/japplphysiol.00587.2005

64. Roth T. Insomnia: Definition, Prevalence, Etiology, and Consequences. *Journal of Clinical Sleep Medicine*. Aug 2007;3(5 suppl):S7-S10. https://doi.org/10.5664/jcsm.26929

65. Jarrin DC, Alvaro PK, Bouchard MA, Jarrin SD, Drake CL, Morin CM. Insomnia and hypertension: A systematic review. *Sleep Medicine Reviews*. Oct 2018;41:3-38. https://doi.org/10.1016/j.smrv.2018.02.003

66. Javaheri S, Redline S. Insomnia and Risk of Cardiovascular Disease. *Chest*. Aug 2017;152(2):435-444. https://doi.org/10.1016/j.chest.2017.01.026

67. Pigeon WR, Bishop TM, Krueger KM. Insomnia as a Precipitating Factor in New Onset Mental Illness: a Systematic Review of Recent Findings. *Current Psychiatry Reports*. Aug 2017;19(8):44. https://doi.org/10.1007/s11920-017-0802-x

68. Riedel BW, Lichstein KL. Insomnia and daytime functioning. *Sleep Medicine Reviews*. Jun 2000;4(3):277-298. https://doi.org/10.1053/smrv.1999.0074

69. Espie CA, Pawlecki B, Waterfield D, Fitton K, Radocchia M, Luik AI. Insomnia symptoms and their association with workplace productivity: cross-sectional and pre-post intervention analyses from a large multinational manufacturing company. *Sleep Health*. Jun 2018;4(3):307-312. https://doi.org/10.1016/j.sleh.2018.03.003

70. Commonwealth of Australia. *Bedtime Reading: A report from the Inquiry into Sleep Health Awareness in Australia*. Apr 2019. Accessed 07/10/2024. https://www.aph.gov.au/Parliamentary_Business/Committees/House/Health_Aged_Care_and_Sport/SleepHealthAwareness/Report

71. Pallesen S, Bjorvatn B, Waage S, Harris A, Sagoe D. Prevalence of Shift Work Disorder: A Systematic Review and Meta-Analysis. *Frontiers in Psychology*. Mar 2021;12:638252. https://doi.org/10.3389/fpsyg.2021.638252

72. Drake CL, Roehrs T, Richardson G, Walsh JK, Roth T. Shift work sleep disorder: Prevalence and consequences beyond that of symptomatic day workers. *Sleep*. Dec 2004;27(8):1453-1462. https://doi.org/10.1093/sleep/27.8.1453

73. Khan Z, Trotti LM. Central disorders of hypersomnolence: Focus on the narcolepsies and idiopathic hypersomnia. *Chest*. Jul 2015;148(1):262-273. https://doi.org/10.1378/chest.14-1304

74. Fleetham JA, Fleming JA. Parasomnias. *Candian Medical Association Journal*. May 2014;186(8):E273-280. https://doi.org/10.1503/cmaj.120808

75. Postuma RB, Montplaisir JY, Pelletier A, et al. Environmental risk factors for REM sleep behavior disorder: a multicenter case-control study. *Neurology*. Jul 2012;79(5):428-434. https://doi.org/10.1212/WNL.0b013e31825dd383

76. Yap AU, Chua AP. Sleep bruxism: Current knowledge and contemporary management. *Journal of Conservative Dentistry*. Sep-Oct 2016;19(5):383-389. https://doi.org/10.4103/0972-0707.190007

77. Lamond N, Dawson D. Quantifying the performance impairment associated with fatigue. *Journal of Sleep Research*. Nov 1999;8(4):255-262. https://doi.org/10.1046/j.1365-2869.1999.00167.x

78. Maisey G, Cattani M, Devine A, Lo J, Fu SC, Dunican IC. Digging for data: How sleep is losing out to roster design, sleep disorders, and lifestyle factors. *Applied Ergonomics*. Feb 2022;99:103617. https://doi.org/10.1016/j.apergo.2021.103617

79. Hossain JL, Reinish LW, Heslegrave RJ, et al. Subjective and Objective Evaluation of Sleep and Performance in Daytime Versus Nighttime Sleep in Extended-Hours Shift-Workers at an Underground Mine. *Journal of Occupational and Environmental Medicine*. Mar 2004;46(3):212-226. https://doi.org/10.1097/01.jom.0000117421.95392.31

80. Lowden A, Kecklund G, Axelsson J, Akerstedt T. Change from an 8-hour shift to a 12-hour shift, attitudes, sleep, sleepiness and performance. *Scandinavian Journal of Work, Environment & Health*. 1998;24(Suppl 3):69-75.

81. Wegrzyn LR, Tamimi RM, Rosner BA, et al. Rotating Night-Shift Work and the Risk of Breast Cancer in the Nurses' Health Studies. *American Journal of Epidemiology*. Sep 2017;186(5):532-540. https://doi.org/10.1093/aje/kwx140

82. Davis S, Mirick DK. Circadian disruption, shift work and the risk of cancer: a summary of the evidence and studies in Seattle. *Cancer Causes & Control*. May 2006;17(4):539-545. https://doi.org/10.1007/s10552-005-9010-9

83. Akerstedt T, Wright KP, Jr. Sleep Loss and Fatigue in Shift Work and Shift Work Disorder. *Sleep Medicine Clinics*. Jun 2009;4(2):257-271. https://doi.org/10.1016/j.jsmc.2009.03.001

84. Nielsen HB, Larsen AD, Dyreborg J, et al. Risk of injury after evening and night work – findings from the Danish Working Hour Database. *Scandinavian Journal of Work, Environment & Health*. Jul 2018;44(4):385-393. https://doi.org/10.5271/sjweh.3737

85. Smith L, Folkard S, Poole CJM. Increased Injuries on Night-Shift. *Lancet*. Oct 1994;344(8930):1137-1139. https://doi.org/10.1016/S0140-6736(94)90636-X

86. Fischer D, Lombardi DA, Folkard S, Willetts J, Christiani DC. Updating the "Risk Index": A systematic review and meta-analysis of occupational injuries and work schedule characteristics. *Chronobiology International*. Oct 2017;34(10):1423-1438. https://doi.org/10.1080/07420528.2017.1367305

87. Folkard S. Do permanent night workers show circadian adjustment? A review based on the endogenous melatonin rhythm. *Chronobiology International*. Apr 2008;25(2):215-224. https://doi.org/10.1080/07420520802106835

88. Barton J, Folkard S, Smith L, Poole CJM. Effects on health of a change from a delaying to an advancing shift system. *Occupational and Environmental Medicine*. 1994;51(11):749-755. https://doi.org/10.1136/oem.51.11.749

89. Shiffer D, Minonzio M, Dipaola F, et al. Effects of Clockwise and Counterclockwise Job Shift Work Rotation on Sleep and Work-Life Balance on Hospital Nurses. *International Journal of Environmental Research and Public Health*. Sep 2018;15(9): 2038. https://doi.org/10.3390/ijerph15092038

90. Shon Y, Ryu S, Suh BS, et al. Comparison of sleep quality based on direction of shift rotation in electronics workers. *Annals of Occupational and Environmental Medicine*. Sep 2016;28(1):37. https://doi.org/10.1186/s40557-016-0122-3

91. McGraw K, Hoffmann R, Harker C, Herman JH. The Development of Circadian Rhythms in a Human Infant. *Sleep*. May 1999;22(3):303-310. https://doi.org/10.1093/sleep/22.3.303

92. Tarokh L, Short M, Crowley SJ, Fontanellaz-Castiglione CEG, Carskadon MA. Sleep and Circadian Rhythms in Adolescence. *Current Sleep Medicine Reports*. Dec 2019;5(4):181-192. https://doi.org/10.1007/s40675-019-00155-w

93. Monk TH. Aging Human Circadian Rhythms: Conventional Wisdom May Not Always Be Right. *Journal of Biological Rhythms*. Aug 2005;20(4):366-374. https://doi.org/10.1177/0748730405277378

94. Härmä MI, Hakola T, Akerstedt T, Laitinen JT. Age and adjustment to night work. *Occupational and Environmental Medicine*. Aug 1994;51(8):568-573. https://doi.org/10.1136/oem.51.8.568

95. Chellappa SL, Bromundt V, Frey S, et al. Association of Intraocular Cataract Lens Replacement With Circadian Rhythms, Cognitive Function, and Sleep in Older Adults. *JAMA Ophthalmology*. May 2019;137(8):878-885. https://doi.org/10.1001/jamaophthalmol.2019.1406

96. Charman WN. Age, lens transmittance, and the possible effects of light on melatonin suppression. *Ophthalmic and Physiological Optics*. Mar 2003;23(2):181-187. https://doi.org/10.1046/j.1475-1313.2003.00105.x

97. Foley DJ, Monjan AA, Brown SL, Simonsick EM, Wallace RB, Blazer DG. Sleep Complaints Among Elderly Persons: An Epidemiologic Study of Three Communities. *Sleep*. Aug 1995;18(6):425-432. https://doi.org/10.1093/sleep/18.6.425

98. Morphy H, Dunn KM, Lewis M, Boardman HF, Croft PR. Epidemiology of Insomnia: a Longitudinal Study in a UK Population. *Sleep*. Mar 2007;30(3):274-280. https://doi.org/10.1093/sleep/30.3.274

99. Young T, Skatrud J, Peppard PE. Risk Factors for Obstructive Sleep Apnea in Adults. *JAMA*. Apr 2004;291(16):2013-2016. https://doi.org/10.1001/jama.291.16.2013

100. Bliwise DL, Foley DJ, Vitiello MV, Ansari FP, Ancoli-Israel S, Walsh JK. Nocturia and disturbed sleep in the elderly. *Sleep Medicine*. May 2009;10(5):540-548. https://doi.org/10.1016/j.sleep.2008.04.002

101. Dupont Rocher S, Bessot N, Sesboüé B, Bulla J, Davenne D. Circadian Characteristics of Older Adults and Aerobic Capacity. *The Journals of Gerontology: Series A*. Jun 2016;71(6):817-22. https://doi.org/10.1093/gerona/glv195

102. Hall SJ, Ferguson SA, Turner AI, Robertson SJ, Vincent GE, Aisbett B. The effect of working on-call on stress physiology and sleep: A systematic review. *Sleep Medicine Reviews*. Jun 2017;33:79-87. https://doi.org/10.1016/j.smrv.2016.06.001

103. Torsvall L, Akerstedt T. Disturbed Sleep While Being on-Call - an EEG Study of Ships' Engineers. *Sleep*. Feb 1988;11(1):35-38. https://doi.org/10.1093/sleep/11.1.35

104. Pilcher JJ, Coplen MK. Work/rest cycles in railroad operations: effects of shorter than 24-h shift work schedules and on-call schedules on sleep. *Ergonomics*. May 2000;43(5):573-588. https://doi.org/10.1080/001401300184260

105. Sprajcer M, Jay SM, Vincent GE, Vakulin A, Lack L, Ferguson SA. How the chance of missing the alarm during an on-call shift affects pre-bed anxiety, sleep and next day cognitive performance. *Biological Psychology*. Sep 2018;137:133-139. https://doi.org/10.1016/j.biopsycho.2018.07.008

106. Ziebertz CM, Beckers DGJ, Van Hooff MLM, Kompier MAJ, Geurts SAE. The effect on sleep of being on-call: an experimental field study. *Journal of Sleep Research*. Mar 2017;26(6):809-815. https://doi.org/10.1111/jsr.12519

107. Imbernon E, Warret G, Roitg C, Chastang JF, Goldberg M. Effects on Health and Social Well-Being of on-Call Shifts - an Epidemiologic-Study in the French National Electricity and Gas Supply Company. *Journal of Occupational and Environmental Medicine*. Nov 1993;35(11):1131-1137. https://doi.org/10.1097/00043764-199311000-00016

108. Wuyts J, De Valck E, Vandekerckhove M, et al. Effects of pre-sleep simulated on-call instructions on subsequent sleep. *Biological Psychology*. Dec 2012;91(3):383-388. https://doi.org/10.1016/j.biopsycho.2012.09.003

109. Sprajcer M, Jay SM, Vincent GE, Vakulin A, Lack L, Ferguson SA. Uncertain call likelihood negatively affects sleep and next-day cognitive performance while on-call in a laboratory environment. *Chronobiology International*. May 2018;35(6):838-848. https://doi.org/10.1080/07420528.2018.1466788

110. United States of America National Aeronautics and Space Administration. *Report to the President: actions to implement the recommendations of the Presidential Commission on the Space Shuttle Challenger Accident*. Jul 1986. Accessed 07/10/2024. https://ntrs.nasa.gov/citations/19860017880

111. Svetieva E, Clerkin C, Ruderman MN. Can't sleep, won't sleep: Exploring leaders' sleep patterns, problems, and attitudes. *Consulting Psychology Journal: Practice and Research*. 2017;69(2):80-97. https://doi.org/10.1037/cpb0000092

112. Barnes CM, Lucianetti L, Bhave DP, Christian MS. "You wouldn't like me when I'm sleepy": Leaders' sleep, daily abusive supervision, and work unit engagement. *Academy of Management Journal*. 2015;58(5):1419-1437. https://doi.org/10.5465/amj.2013.1063

113. Barnes CM, Schaubroeck J, Huth M, Ghumman S. Lack of sleep and unethical conduct. *Organizational Behavior and Human Decision Processes*. Jul 2011;115(2):169-180. https://doi.org/10.1016/j.obhdp.2011.01.009

114. Barnes CM, Guarana CL, Nauman S, Kong DT. Too tired to inspire or be inspired: Sleep deprivation and charismatic leadership. *Journal of Applied Psychology*. Aug 2016;101(8):1191-1199. https://doi.org/10.1037/apl0000123

115. Nowack K. Sleep, emotional intelligence, and interpersonal effectiveness: Natural bedfellows. *Consulting Psychology Journal: Practice and Research*. 2017;69(2):66-79. https://doi.org/10.1037/cpb0000077

116. Guarana CL, Barnes CM. Lack of sleep and the development of leader-follower relationships over time. *Organizational Behavior and Human Decision Processes*. Jul 2017;141:57-73. https://doi.org/10.1016/j.obhdp.2017.04.003

117. Olsen OK, Pallesen S, Torsheim T, Espevik R. The effect of sleep deprivation on leadership behaviour in military officers: an experimental study. *Journal of Sleep Research*. Dec 2016;25(6):683-689. https://doi.org/10.1111/jsr.12431

118. Thomas MJW, Gupta CC, Sprajcer M, et al. *Fatigue and Driving: An International Review*. Sep 2021. Accessed 07/10/2024. https://www.aaa.asn.au/wp-content/uploads/2021/10/Fatigue-Driving-Literature-Review-FINAL.pdf

119. Åkerstedt T, Peters B, Anund A, Kecklund G. Impaired alertness and performance driving home from the night shift: a driving simulator study. *Journal of Sleep Research*. Mar 2005;14(1):17-20. https://doi.org/10.1111/j.1365-2869.2004.00437.x

120. Larue G, Rakotonirainy A, Pettitt AN. Driving performance impairments due to hypovigilance on monotonous roads. *Accident Analysis & Prevention*. Nov 2011;43(6):2037-2046. https://doi.org/10.1016/j.aap.2011.05.023

121. Blaivas AJ, Patel R, Hom D, Antigua K, Ashtyani H. Quantifying microsleep to help assess subjective sleepiness. *Sleep Medicine*. Mar 2007;8(2):156-159. https://doi.org/10.1016/j.sleep.2006.06.011

122. Zaky MH, Shoorangiz R, Poudel GR, Yang L, Innes CRH, Jones RD. Increased cerebral activity during microsleeps reflects an unconscious drive to re-establish consciousness. *International Journal of Psychophysiology*. Jul 2023;189:57-65. https://doi.org/10.1016/j.ijpsycho.2023.05.349

123. Reilly T, Atkinson G, Waterhouse J. Travel fatigue and jet-lag. *Journal of Sports Sciences*. 1997;15(3):365-369. https://doi.org/10.1080/026404197367371

124. Samuels CH. Jet Lag and Travel Fatigue: A Comprehensive Management Plan for Sport Medicine Physicians and High-Performance Support Teams. *Clinical Journal of Sport Medicine*. May 2012;22(3):268-273. https://doi.org/10.1097/JSM.0b013e31824d2eeb

125. Lastella M, Roach GD, Sargent C. Travel fatigue and sleep/wake behaviors of professional soccer players during international competition. *Sleep Health*. Apr 2019;5(2):141-147. https://doi.org/10.1016/j.sleh.2018.10.013

126. Waterhouse J, Reilly T, Edwards B. The stress of travel. *Journal of Sports Sciences*. Oct 2004;22(10):946-65. https://doi.org/10.1080/02640410400000264

127. Sateia MJ. International classification of sleep disorders-third edition: highlights and modifications. *Chest*. Nov 2014;146(5):1387-1394. https://doi.org/10.1378/chest.14-0970

128. Arendt J, Skene DJ. Melatonin as a chronobiotic. *Sleep Medicine Reviews*. Feb 2005;9(1):25-39. https://doi.org/10.1016/j.smrv.2004.05.002

129. Zhdanova IV. Melatonin as a hypnotic: Pro. *Sleep Medicine Reviews*. Feb 2005;9(1):51-65. https://doi.org/10.1016/j.smrv.2004.04.003

130. Eastman CI, Burgess HJ. How to travel the world without jet lag. *Sleep Medicine Clinics*. Jun 2009;4(2):241-255. https://doi.org/10.1016/j.jsmc.2009.02.006

131. Roach GD, Sargent C. Interventions to Minimize Jet Lag After Westward and Eastward Flight. *Frontiers in Physiology*. Jul 2019;10. https://doi.org/10.3389/fphys.2019.00927

132. Burke TM, Markwald RR, McHill AW, et al. Effects of caffeine on the human circadian clock in vivo and in vitro. *Science Translational Medicine*. Sep 2015;7(305):305ra146-305ra146. https://doi.org/10.1126/scitranslmed.aac5125

133. Piérard C, Beaumont M, Enslen M, et al. Resynchronization of hormonal rhythms after an eastbound flight in humans: effects of slow-release caffeine and melatonin. *European Journal of Applied Physiology*. Jul 2001;85:144-150. https://doi.org/10.1007/s004210100418

134. Armstrong LE, Pumerantz AC, Roti MW, et al. Fluid, electrolyte, and renal indices of hydration during 11 days of controlled caffeine consumption. *International Journal of Sport Nutrition and Exercise Metabolism*. 2005;15(3):252-265. https://doi.org/10.1123/ijsnem.15.3.252

135. Halson SL, Burke LM, Pearce J. Nutrition for Travel: From Jet lag To Catering. *International Journal of Sport Nutrition and Exercise Metabolism*. Mar 2019;29(2):228-235. https://doi.org/10.1123/ijsnem.2018-0278

136. Janse van Rensburg DCC, Fowler P, Racinais S. Practical tips to manage travel fatigue and jet lag in athletes. *British Journal of Sports Medicine*; Aug 2021;55:821-822. https://doi.org/10.1136/bjsports-2020-103163

137. Waterhouse J, Reilly T, Atkinson G, Edwards B. Jet lag: trends and coping strategies. *The Lancet*. Mar 2007;369(9567):1117-1129. https://doi.org/10.1016/S0140-6736(07)60529-7

138. Garcia AN, Salloum IM. Polysomnographic sleep disturbances in nicotine, caffeine, alcohol, cocaine, opioid, and cannabis use: a focused review. *The American Journal on Addictions*. Oct 2015;24(7):590-598. https://doi.org/10.1111/ajad.12291

139. Caldwell Jr JA, Caldwell JL. Comparison of the effects of zolpidem-induced prophylactic naps to placebo naps and forced rest periods in prolonged work schedules. *Sleep*. Jan 1998;21(1):79-90. https://doi.org/10.1093/sleep/21.1.79

140. Dooley M, Plosker GL. Zaleplon: a review of its use in the treatment of insomnia. *Drugs*. Sep 2000;60(2):413-445. https://doi.org/10.2165/00003495-200060020-00014

141. Whitmore JN, Fischer Jr JR, Storm WF. Hypnotic efficacy of zaleplon for daytime sleep in rested individuals. *Sleep*. Aug 2004;27(5):895-898. https://doi.org/10.1093/sleep/27.5.895

142. Lemmer B. The sleep–wake cycle and sleeping pills. *Physiology & Behavior*. Feb 2007;90(2-3):285-293. https://doi.org/10.1016/j.physbeh.2006.09.006

143. Dorrian J, Skinner N. Alcohol Consumption Patterns of Shiftworkers Compared With Dayworkers. *Chronobiology International*. Jun 2012;29(5):610-618. https://doi.org/10.3109/07420528.2012.675848

144. Richter K, Peter L, Rodenbeck A, Weess HG, Riedel-Heller SG, Hillemacher T. Shiftwork and Alcohol Consumption: A Systematic Review of the Literature. *European Addiction Research*. Jan 2021;27(1):9-15. https://doi.org/10.1159/000507573

145. Finan PH, Goodin BR, Smith MT. The association of sleep and pain: an update and a path forward. *The Journal of Pain*. Dec 2013;14(12):1539-1552. https://doi.org/10.1016/j.jpain.2013.08.007

146. Haack M, Mullington JM. Sustained sleep restriction reduces emotional and physical well-being. *Pain*. Dec 2005;119(1-3):56-64. https://doi.org/10.1016/j.pain.2005.09.011

147. Roehrs T, Hyde M, Blaisdell B, Greenwald M, Roth T. Sleep loss and REM sleep loss are hyperalgesic. *Sleep*. Feb 2006;29(2):145-151. https://doi.org/10.1093/sleep/29.2.145

148. Cannizzaro E, Cirrincione L, Mazzucco W, et al. Night-Time Shift Work and Related Stress Responses: A Study on Security Guards. *International Journal of Environmental Research and Public Health*. Jan 2020;17(2): 562. https://doi.org/10.3390/ijerph17020562

149. Gerber M, Hartmann T, Brand S, Holsboer-Trachsler E, Pühse U. The relationship between shift work, perceived stress, sleep and health in Swiss police officers. *Journal of Criminal Justice*. Nov-Dec 2010;38(6):1167-1175. https://doi.org/10.1016/j.jcrimjus.2010.09.005

150. Malak MZ, Al-Amer RM, Abu Adas MH. The influence of shift-work on perceived stress, sleep quality, and body mass index among emergency nurses. *Journal of Human Behavior in the Social Environment*. Aug 2023;33(6):779-792. https://doi.org/10.1080/10911359.2023.2177226

151. Gardiner C, Weakley J, Burke LM, et al. The effect of caffeine on subsequent sleep: A systematic review and meta-analysis. *Sleep Medicine Reviews*. Jun 2023;69:101764. https://doi.org/10.1016/j.smrv.2023.101764

152. Boege HL, Bhatti MZ, St-Onge MP. Circadian rhythms and meal timing: impact on energy balance and body weight. *Current Opinion in Biotechnology*. Aug 2021;70:1-6. https://doi.org/10.1016/j.copbio.2020.08.009

153. Baron KG, Reid KJ, Kern AS, Zee PC. Role of sleep timing in caloric intake and BMI. *Obesity*. Jul 2011;19(7):1374-1381. https://doi.org/10.1038/oby.2011.100

154. Spaeth AM, Hawley NL, Raynor HA, et al. Sleep, energy balance, and meal timing in school-aged children. *Sleep Medicine*. Aug 2019;60:139-144. https://doi.org/10.1016/j.sleep.2019.02.003

155. Thomas EA, Zaman A, Cornier MA, et al. Later Meal and Sleep Timing Predicts Higher Percent Body Fat. *Nutrients*. Dec 2020;13(1): 73. https://doi.org/10.3390/nu13010073

156. Kervezee L, Kosmadopoulos A, Boivin DB. Metabolic and cardiovascular consequences of shift work: The role of circadian disruption and sleep disturbances. *European Journal of Neuroscience*. Jan 2020;51(1):396-412. https://doi.org/10.1111/ejn.14216

157. Parsons MJ, Moffitt TE, Gregory AM, et al. Social jetlag, obesity and metabolic disorder: investigation in a cohort study. *International Journal of Obesity*. May 2015;39(5):842-848. https://doi.org/10.1038/ijo.2014.201

158. Zeron-Rugerio MF, Hernaez A, Porras-Loaiza AP, Cambras T, Izquierdo-Pulido M. Eating Jet Lag: A Marker of the Variability in Meal Timing and Its Association

with Body Mass Index. *Nutrients*. Dec 2019;11(12): 2980. https://doi.org/10.3390/nu11122980

159. Hirshkowitz M, Whiton K, Albert SM, et al. National Sleep Foundation's sleep time duration recommendations: methodology and results summary. *Sleep Health*. Mar 2015;1(1):40-43. https://doi.org/10.1016/j.sleh.2014.12.010

160. Gupta CC, Centofanti S, Dorrian J, et al. Altering meal timing to improve cognitive performance during simulated nightshifts. *Chronobiology International*. Dec 2019;36(12):1691-1713. https://doi.org/10.1080/07420528.2019.1676256

161. Maddison KJ, Kosky C, Walsh JH. Is There a Place for Medicinal Cannabis in Treating Patients with Sleep Disorders? What We Know so Far. *Nature and Science of Sleep*. 2022;14:957-968. https://doi.org/10.2147/NSS.S340949

162. Walsh JH, Maddison KJ, Rankin T, et al. Treating insomnia symptoms with medicinal cannabis: a randomized, crossover trial of the efficacy of a cannabinoid medicine compared with placebo. *Sleep*. Nov 2021;44(11): zsab149. https://doi.org/10.1093/sleep/zsab149

163. Prather AA, Hall M, Fury JM, et al. Sleep and Antibody Response to Hepatitis B Vaccination. *Sleep*. Aug 2012;35(8):1063-1069. https://doi.org/10.5665/sleep.1990

164. Besedovsky L, Lange T, Haack M. The Sleep-Immune Crosstalk in Health and Disease. *Physiological Reviews*. Jul 2019;99(3):1325-1380. https://doi.org/10.1152/physrev.00010.2018

165. Spiegel K, Sheridan JF, Van Cauter E. Effect of sleep deprivation on response to immunization. *JAMA*. Sep 2002;288(12):1471-1472. https://doi.org/10.1001/jama.288.12.1471-a

166. Cohen S, Doyle WJ, Alper CM, Janicki-Deverts D, Turner RB. Sleep Habits and Susceptibility to the Common Cold. *Archives of Internal Medicine*. Jan 2009;169(1):62-67. https://doi.org/10.1001/archinternmed.2008.505

167. Lange T, Dimitrov S, Bollinger T, Diekelmann S, Born J. Sleep after Vaccination Boosts Immunological Memory. *The Journal of Immunology*. Jul 2011;187(1):283-290. https://doi.org/10.4049/jimmunol.1100015

168. Chauvineau M, Pasquier F, Guyot V, Aloulou A, Nedelec M. Effect of the Depth of Cold Water Immersion on Sleep Architecture and Recovery Among Well-Trained Male Endurance Runners. *Frontiers in Sports and Active Living*. Mar 2021;3:659990. https://doi.org/10.3389/fspor.2021.659990

169. Arab A, Rafie N, Amani R, Shirani F. The Role of Magnesium in Sleep Health: a Systematic Review of Available Literature. *Biological Trace Element Research*. Feb 2023;201(1):121-128. doi:10.1007/s12011-022-03162-1

170. Avni T, Reich S, Lev N, Gafter-Gvili A. Iron supplementation for restless legs syndrome - A systematic review and meta-analysis. *European Journal of Internal Medicine*. May 2019;63:34-41. https://doi.org/10.1016/j.ejim.2019.02.009

171. Exelmans L, Van den Bulck J. Technology and Sleep: How Electronic Media Exposure Has Impacted Core Concepts of Sleep Medicine. *Behavioral Sleep Medicine*. Sep 2015;13(6):439-441. https://doi.org/10.1080/15402002.2015.1083025

172. Cajochen C, Frey S, Anders D, et al. Evening exposure to a light-emitting diodes (LED)-backlit computer screen affects circadian physiology and cognitive performance. *Journal of Applied Physiology*. May 2011;110(5):1432-1438. https://doi.org/10.1152/japplphysiol.00165.2011

173. Wood B, Rea MS, Plitnick B, Figueiro MG. Light level and duration of exposure determine the impact of self-luminous tablets on melatonin suppression. *Applied Ergonomics*. Mar 2013;44(2):237-240. https://doi.org/10.1016/j.apergo.2012.07.008

174. Phillips AJK, Vidafar P, Burns AC, et al. High sensitivity and interindividual variability in the response of the human circadian system to evening light. *Proceedings of the National Academy of Sciences*. May 2019;116(24):12019-12024. https://doi.org/10.1073/pnas.1901824116

175. Higuchi S, Motohashi Y, Liu Y, Maeda A. Effects of playing a computer game using a bright display on presleep physiological variables, sleep latency, slow wave sleep and REM sleep. *Journal of Sleep Research*. Sep 2005;14(3):267-273. https://doi.org/10.1111/j.1365-2869.2005.00463.x

176. Grønli J, Byrkjedal KI, Bjorvatn B, Nødtvedt Ø, Hamre B, Pallesen S. Reading from an iPad or from a book in bed: the impact on human sleep. a randomized controlled crossover trial. *Sleep Medicine*. May 2016;21:86-92. https://doi.org/10.1016/j.sleep.2016.02.006

177. Cajochen C, Stefani O, Schöllhorn I, Lang D, Chellappa SL. Influence of evening light exposure on polysomnographically assessed night-time sleep: A systematic review with meta-analysis. *Lighting Research & Technology*. Oct 2022;54(6):609-624. https://doi.org/10.1177/14771535221078765

178. Bauducco S, Pillion M, Bartel K, Reynolds C, Kahn M, Gradisar M. A bidirectional model of sleep and technology use: A theoretical review of How much, for whom, and which mechanisms. *Sleep Medicine Reviews*. Aug 2024;76:101933. https://doi.org/10.1016/j.smrv.2024.101933

179. Weaver E, Gradisar M, Dohnt H, Lovato N, Douglas P. The effect of presleep video-game playing on adolescent sleep. *Journal of Clinical Sleep Medicine*. Apr 2010;6(2):184-189. https://doi.org/10.5664/jcsm.27769

180. Combertaldi SL, Ort A, Cordi M, Fahr A, Rasch B. Pre-sleep social media use does not strongly disturb sleep: a sleep laboratory study in healthy young participants. *Sleep Medicine*. Nov 2021;87:191-202. https://doi.org/10.1016/j.sleep.2021.09.009

181. Pallesen S, Larsen S, Bjorvatn B. "I Wish I'd Slept Better in That Hotel"—Guests' Self-reported Sleep Patterns in Hotels. *Scandinavian Journal of Hospitality and Tourism*. Aug 2016;16(3):243-253. https://doi.org/10.1080/15022250.2015.1074938

182. Mao Z, Yang Y, Wang M. Sleepless nights in hotels? Understanding factors that influence hotel sleep quality. *International Journal of Hospitality Management*. Aug 2018;74:189-201. https://doi.org/10.1016/j.ijhm.2018.05.002

183. Xiong W, Huang M, Okumus B, Fan F. Rethinking sleep quality in hotels: examining the risk and protective factors associated with travel-related insomnia. *International Journal of Hospitality Management*. Sep 2020;90:102644. https://doi.org/10.1016/j.ijhm.2020.102644

184. Robbins R, Grandner M, Knowlden A, Severt K. Examining key hotel attributes for guest sleep and overall satisfaction. *Tourism and Hospitality Research*. Apr 2021;21(2):144-155. https://doi.org/10.1177/1467358420961544

185. Sletten TL, Weaver MD, Foster RG, et al. The importance of sleep regularity: a consensus statement of the National Sleep Foundation sleep timing and variability panel. *Sleep Health*. Dec 2023;9(6):801-820. https://doi.org/10.1016/j.sleh.2023.07.016

186. Dittami J, Keckeis M, Machatschke I, Katina S, Zeitlhofer J, Kloesch G. Sex differences in the reactions to sleeping in pairs versus sleeping alone in humans. *Sleep and Biological Rhythms*. Oct 2007;5(4):271-276. https://doi.org/10.1111/j.1479-8425.2007.00320.x

187. Meadows R, Venn S, Hislop J, Stanley N, Arber S. Investigating couples' sleep: an evaluation of actigraphic analysis techniques. *Journal of Sleep Research*. Dec 2005;14(4):377-386. https://doi.org/10.1111/j.1365-2869.2005.00485.x

188. Chin BN, Singh T, Carothers AS. Co-sleeping with pets, stress, and sleep in a nationally-representative sample of United States adults. *Scientific Reports*. Mar 2024;14(1):5577. I https://doi.org/10.1038/s41598-024-56055-9

189. Andre CJ, Lovallo V, Spencer RM. The effects of bed sharing on sleep: From partners to pets. *Sleep Health*. Jun 2021;7(3):314-323. https://doi.org/10.1016/j.sleh.2020.11.011

190. Frazier TW, Krishna J, Klingemier E, Beukemann M, Nawabit R, Ibrahim S. A Randomized, Crossover Trial of a Novel Sound-to-Sleep Mattress Technology in Children with Autism and Sleep Difficulties. *Journal of Clinical Sleep Medicine*. Jan 15 2017;13(1):95-104. https://doi.org/10.5664/jcsm.6398

191. Chiba S, Yagi T, Ozone M, et al. High rebound mattress toppers facilitate core body temperature drop and enhance deep sleep in the initial phase of nocturnal sleep. *PLoS One*. Jun 2018;13(6):e0197521. https://doi.org/10.1371/journal.pone.0197521

192. Bidarian-Moniri A, Nilsson M, Attia J, Ejnell H. Mattress and pillow for prone positioning for treatment of obstructive sleep apnoea. *Acta Oto-Laryngologica*. Mar 2015;135(3):271-276. https://doi.org/10.3109/00016489.2014.968674

193. Richard W, Venker J, den Herder C, et al. Acceptance and long-term compliance of nCPAP in obstructive sleep apnea. *European Archives of Oto-Rhino-Laryngology*. Sep 2007;264(9):1081-1086. https://doi.org/10.1007/s00405-007-0311-3

194. Williamson AA, Mindell J, Cicalese O, Varker A, Carson M. A social media analysis about the use and efficacy of alternative child sleep aids [Conference Abstract]. *Pediatrics*. Mar 2021;147(3_MeetingAbstract):1-2. https://doi.org/10.1542/peds.147.3MA1.1b

195. Becklund AL, Rapp-McCall L, Nudo J. Using weighted blankets in an inpatient mental health hospital to decrease anxiety. *Journal of Integrative Medicine*. Mar 2021;19(2):129-134. https://doi.org/10.1016/j.joim.2020.11.004

196. Novak T, Scanlan J, McCaul D, MacDonald N, Clarke T. Pilot study of a sensory room in an acute inpatient psychiatric unit. *Australasian Psychiatry*. Oct 2012;20(5):401-406. https://doi.org/10.1177/1039856212459585

197. Hjort Telhede E, Arvidsson S, Karlsson S. Nursing staff's experiences of how weighted blankets influence resident's in nursing homes expressions of health. *International Journal of Qualitative Studies on Health and Well-being*. Dec 2022;17(1):2009203. https://doi.org/10.1080/17482631.2021.2009203

198. Vinson J, Powers J, Mosesso K. Weighted Blankets: Anxiety Reduction in Adult Patients Receiving Chemotherapy. *Clinical Journal of Oncology Nursing*. Aug 1 2020;24(4):360-368. https://doi.org/10.1188/20.cjon.360-368

199. Summe V, Baker RB, Eichel MM. Safety, Feasibility, and Effectiveness of Weighted Blankets in the Care of Infants With Neonatal Abstinence Syndrome: A Crossover Randomized Controlled Trial. *Advances in Neonatal Care*. Oct 2020;20(5):384-391. https://doi.org/10.1097/anc.0000000000000724

200. Gee BM, Lloyd K, Sutton J, McOmber T. Weighted Blankets and Sleep Quality in Children with Autism Spectrum Disorders: A Single-Subject Design. *Children*. Dec 2020;8(1):10. https://doi.org/10.3390/children8010010

201. Gringras P, Green D, Wright B, et al. Weighted blankets and sleep in autistic children - A randomized controlled trial. *Pediatrics*. Aug 2014;134(2):298-306. https://doi.org/10.1542/peds.2013-4285

202. Larsson I, Aili K, Nygren JM, Jarbin H, Svedberg P. Parents' Experiences of Weighted Blankets' Impact on Children with Attention-Deficit/Hyperactivity Disorder (ADHD) and Sleep Problems-A Qualitative Study. *International Journal of Environmental Research and Public Health*. Dec 2021;18(24):12959. https://doi.org/10.3390/ijerph182412959

203. Danoff-Burg S, Rus HM, Cruz Martir L, Raymann RJ. Worth the weight: Weighted blanket improves sleep and increases relaxation [Conference Abstract]. *Sleep*. Apr 2020;43(Suppl 1):A460. https://doi.org/10.1093/sleep/zsaa056.1197

204. Baumgartner JN, Quintana D, Leija L, et al. Widespread Pressure Delivered by a Weighted Blanket Reduces Chronic Pain: A Randomized Controlled Trial. *The Journal of Pain*. Jan 2022;23(1):156-174. https://doi.org/10.1016/j.jpain.2021.07.009

205. Goines L, Hagler L. Noise pollution: a modem plague. *Southern Medical Journal*. Mar 2007;100(3):287-94. https://doi.org/10.1097/smj.0b013e3180318be5

206. Halperin D. Environmental noise and sleep disturbances: A threat to health? *Sleep Science*. Dec 2014;7(4):209-212. https://doi.org/10.1016/j.slsci.2014.11.003

207. Simonelli G, Dudley KA, Weng J, et al. Neighborhood Factors as Predictors of Poor Sleep in the Sueño Ancillary Study of the Hispanic Community Health Study/Study of Latinos. *Sleep*. Jan 2017;40(1):zsw025. https://doi.org/10.1093/sleep/zsw025

208. Griefahn B, Marks A, Robens S. Noise emitted from road, rail and air traffic and their effects on sleep. *Journal of Sound and Vibration*. Aug 2006;295(1):129-140. https://doi.org/10.1016/j.jsv.2005.12.052

209. Thacher JD, Poulsen AH, Raaschou-Nielsen O, et al. Exposure to transportation noise and risk for cardiovascular disease in a nationwide cohort study from Denmark. *Environmental Research*. Aug 2022;211:113106. https://doi.org/10.1016/j.envres.2022.113106

210. Selander J, Bluhm G, Theorell T, et al. Saliva cortisol and exposure to aircraft noise in six European countries. *Environmental Health Perspectives*. Nov 2009;117(11):1713-1717. https://doi.org/10.1289/ehp.0900933

211. Lillehei AS, Halcon LL. A systematic review of the effect of inhaled essential oils on sleep. *The Journal of Alternative and Complementary Medicine*. Jun 2014;20(6):441-451. https://doi.org/10.1089/acm.2013.031

212. Fismer KL, Pilkington K. Lavender and sleep: A systematic review of the evidence. *European Journal of Integrative Medicine*. 2012;4(4):e436-e447. https://doi.org/10.1016/j.eujim.2012.08.001

213. Lee M-k, Lim S, Song J-A, Kim M-E, Hur M-H. The effects of aromatherapy essential oil inhalation on stress, sleep quality and immunity in healthy adults: Randomized controlled trial. *European Journal of Integrative Medicine*. Jun 2017;12:79-86. https://doi.org/10.1016/j.eujim.2017.04.009

www.ingramcontent.com/pod-product-compliance
Lightning Source LLC
Chambersburg PA
CBHW080614270326
41928CB00016B/3056